Microsoft Flight Simulator 2024 Game Guide

Navigate Like a Pro: From First-Time Pilot to Advanced Aviator

Kevin O. Samson

Copyright © 2024 by Kevin O. Samson
All rights reserved.

No part of this publication may be reproduced, distributed, or transmitted in any form or by any means, including photocopying, recording, or other electronic or mechanical methods, without the prior written permission of the publisher, except in the case of brief quotations embodied in critical reviews and certain other non-commercial uses permitted by copyright law. For permission requests, write to the publisher at the address below

Disclaimer

The information contained in this book is for general informational purposes only. While every effort has been made to ensure the accuracy of the content, the author, publisher, and any associated parties do not guarantee the accuracy, completeness, or timeliness of the information provided. *Mastering Microsoft Flight Simulator 2024* is a guide and reference to help readers improve their skills in *Microsoft Flight Simulator 2024*, and the content is based on the version of the software available at the time of publication.

This book is **not** affiliated with or endorsed by Microsoft Corporation, Asobo Studio, or any other entity involved in the development of *Microsoft Flight Simulator 2024*. The trademarks and copyrights associated with *Microsoft Flight Simulator 2024* are owned by their respective companies.

No Liability: The author and publisher shall not be liable for any damages or losses, including but not limited to any technical or software-related issues, that may arise from the use of the information or advice presented in this book. Readers are encouraged to use their discretion when implementing the strategies, tips, and techniques provided.

Third-Party Content: The book may mention third-party websites, software, or add-ons. These are provided solely for convenience and informational purposes. The author and publisher do not control or endorse these external sites or products, and are not responsible for their content or performance.

By using this book, the reader agrees to hold the author and publisher harmless for any consequences or issues that may arise from its use.

Table of contents

INTRODUCTION 8

CHAPTER 1 16
   NEW HORIZONS: WHAT'S NEW IN MSFS 2024? 16
      New Aircraft, Maps, and Technical Innovations 16
      Expanded Maps: Explore the World in Detail 18
      Updated Real-World Data and Graphics Enhancements 21
   GAMEPLAY ESSENTIALS 24
      Getting Started: Your First Flight 24
      Quick Start Guide for New Pilots 29

CHAPTER 2 33
   MASTERING THE CONTROLS 33
      Basic Controls for Beginners 33
      Advanced Settings for Sim Pilots 36

CHAPTER 3 42
   CAMERA & VIEW MODES: FINDING YOUR PERFECT VIEW 42
      Cockpit, Exterior, and Drone Camera Options 42
      Customizing Camera Angles for Better Control 46
      All About Aircraft: Your Flying Machines 50
      Military and Special Aircraft 55

CHAPTER 4 59
   PERSONALIZING YOUR AIRCRAFT 59
      Livery Customization and Modding Options 59
   FLIGHT TECHNIQUES & TUTORIALS 68
      How to Take Off, Fly, and Land Like a Pro 70
      Handling Weather and Environmental Factors 74

CHAPTER 5 77
   ADVANCED FLIGHT TECHNIQUES 77
      Navigating Using IFR (Instrument Flight Rules) 77
      Flying in VFR (Visual Flight Rules) 80
      Managing Autopilot and Complex Flight Systems 82

CHAPTER 6 .... **85**

EMERGENCY PROCEDURES: HANDLING IN-GAME CRISES 85
  What to Do in Case of Engine Failures *85*
  What to Do in Case of Turbulence *88*
  What to Do in Case of Storms *90*

CHAPTER 7 .... **94**

EXPLORATION & MISSIONS 94
  Explore the World: The Ultimate Flight Experience *94*
  Discovering Iconic Landmarks and Cities *96*

CHAPTER 8 .... **102**

MISSIONS & CHALLENGES: TAKING YOUR SKILLS FURTHER 102
  Earning Rewards and Completing Objectives *105*
  Flying with Friends: Multiplayer Mode *109*
  Connecting with Fellow Pilots Online *111*
  Participating in Live Events and Global Challenges *113*

CHAPTER 9 .... **116**

LIVE WEATHER AND REAL-WORLD TRAFFIC 116
  Enhancing Your Flight with Real-World Data *116*
  How to Maximize Your Immersion Using Live Features *119*

CHAPTER 10 .... **123**

TRAINING & FLIGHT SCHOOL 123
  Interactive Training: A Step-by-Step Learning Experience *123*
  Mastering Your First Solo Flight *125*
  Specialized Lessons for Different Aircraft and Maneuvers *127*

CHAPTER 11 .... **131**

ADVANCED FLIGHT SCHOOLS AND ADD-ONS 131
  Third-Party Content for Expert Pilots *131*
  How to Access Extra Training Modules and Resources *134*

CHAPTER 12 .... **138**

EXPERT TIPS, TRICKS, & SECRETS 138
  Pro Tips: Becoming a Master Pilot *138*
  Expert Strategies for Navigation, Smooth Landings, and More *140*

Hidden Features and Easter Eggs 142
CHAPTER 13 .... **146**
 TROUBLESHOOTING & FAQS 146
  Technical Support: Solving Common Issues 146
  Optimizing Game Performance 148
  Resolving Controller and Setup Problems 150
  Frequently Asked Questions (FAQs) 152
CONCLUSION & FINAL THOUGHTS **155**

Introduction

Welcome to Microsoft Flight Simulator 2024

Welcome aboard the most immersive, realistic, and visually breathtaking flight simulation experience ever created. *Microsoft Flight Simulator 2024* continues the legacy of its predecessors, setting the bar for virtual aviation enthusiasts around the world. Whether you're a seasoned pilot or a first-time flyer, this game offers a comprehensive experience designed to cater to every type of player.

From the moment you lift off, you'll be greeted with stunningly realistic landscapes, detailed aircraft, and an expansive, fully realized world to explore. *Microsoft Flight Simulator 2024* allows you to experience the thrill of flying not only as a pilot but as an adventurer exploring an ever-evolving world.

Whether you want to soar above iconic landmarks, master the complexities of real-world aviation, or take on challenging flight missions, this game is your gateway to a new world of flying.

Game Overview

Microsoft Flight Simulator 2024 brings an unprecedented level of realism and detail to the genre, allowing players to experience the world from the skies like never before. With the continued use of satellite imagery, AI-powered environmental systems, and real-world data, it offers a flight experience that feels genuinely authentic.

Key Features:

- **Realistic Flight Dynamics**: Every aircraft in the game, from the tiniest single-engine plane to massive airliners, behaves realistically based on their true-to-life flight dynamics. Every control surface and system can be fine-tuned, and the physics engine responds in real-time to atmospheric changes, ensuring that every takeoff, landing, and maneuver feels accurate.

- **Stunning Visuals**: Powered by the latest in graphical technology, *Microsoft Flight Simulator 2024* features stunning landscapes, accurate cityscapes, and faithfully recreated terrain. This includes real-world weather systems, dynamic cloud formations, and time-of-day cycles that change how each flight feels.

- **Dynamic World**: The game's world is powered by live data, meaning every flight you take is influenced by real-time information. The world's weather, traffic, and events evolve as the day progresses, bringing fresh challenges to pilots.

- **Advanced AI and Real-World Data Integration**: The game utilizes AI to simulate complex air traffic, including live commercial flights that mimic real-world schedules. By tapping into real-world data, *Microsoft Flight Simulator 2024* also offers live weather, environmental effects, and air traffic, ensuring no two flights are ever alike.

- **Mission Variety**: The game includes a variety of missions and challenges ranging from long-haul flights, aerobatic stunts, to search and rescue operations. Each mission is tailored to help players of different skill levels grow their aviation expertise.

- **Cockpit and System Interactivity**: The game's aircraft are designed to be as interactive as possible. For enthusiasts of complex systems, the full functionality of cockpits, navigation systems, and flight controls can be accessed, from operating autopilot systems to manually controlling engines and hydraulic systems.

Key Features and Advancements

Microsoft Flight Simulator 2024 builds on the success of its predecessors by introducing a variety of exciting new features, improvements, and advancements that further refine the experience for players.

1. Enhanced Visual Fidelity:

- The visuals in *Microsoft Flight Simulator 2024* are more stunning than ever, with improved lighting effects, sharper textures, and photogrammetry technology for more accurate 3D models of cities and landmarks. These updates make flying through major cities like New York, Paris, or Tokyo feel lifelike and incredibly immersive.

2. New Aircraft and Enhanced Flight Models:

- Players can explore new aircraft types, including some rare or iconic planes. The flight models have been significantly refined, offering even more realism when controlling aircraft. Whether you're piloting a small Cessna or a Boeing 747, the game's flight physics and cockpit systems reflect accurate, real-world aircraft behavior.

3. AI-Powered Dynamic Weather:

- Weather is now more dynamic than ever. The in-game weather system is powered by AI, providing true-to-life forecasting, including turbulence, thunderstorms, and cloud systems. Pilots can adjust to sudden weather changes, adding a layer of challenge and realism.

4. Expanded Training System:

- New interactive flight training sessions have been added, allowing players to learn everything from basic maneuvers to advanced flight planning techniques. The training modules are designed for pilots at any skill level, and they include practical lessons with realistic feedback and tips.

5. Real-Time Air Traffic and Multiplayer Updates:

- The multiplayer features have been expanded, allowing players to fly in real time alongside other pilots. Air traffic is now more realistic, featuring real-world flights as AI traffic, making every flight feel like a part of the global aviation network.

6. Aircraft Customization:

- MSFS 2024 introduces more customization options for aircraft. You can now modify cockpit layouts, change aircraft liveries, and even adjust the performance settings to match your flying style, giving you a deeper level of control over your aviation experience.

7. Expanded Global Scenery:

- The game's world map is vast and includes more intricate details, with updates in remote areas and newly mapped territories, including more detailed oceans, lakes, and mountain ranges. Players can explore and fly anywhere, experiencing highly detailed topographies and cities.

8. Improved Controller Support:

- Whether you prefer using a joystick, flight yoke, or gamepad, *Microsoft Flight Simulator 2024* offers improved support for all controller types. It's now easier than ever to tailor the controls to your preference, enhancing the overall flying experience.

Platform Support: PC, Xbox, and Beyond

Microsoft Flight Simulator 2024 is available on multiple platforms, allowing a wide range of players to experience the world of aviation.

PC Version:

- For PC players, *Microsoft Flight Simulator 2024* offers the most immersive and customizable experience. With support for high-end gaming PCs, players can take advantage of ultra-high-definition graphics, ultra-wide monitors, and the latest in VR technology. The PC version also supports a range of peripherals such as flight sticks, yokes, pedals, and other specialized equipment to enhance the experience.

- **Recommended System Requirements**: To get the most out of the game, players will need a high-performance system, with the ability to run the game at a smooth frame rate while handling the detailed textures and large environments. The game recommends a multi-core processor, a modern graphics card (like the NVIDIA RTX series), and at least 16GB of RAM for optimal performance.

Xbox Series X|S Version:

- The game has been optimized for Xbox Series X|S, offering smooth and responsive gameplay at 4K resolution on the Series X and a balanced experience on the Series S. The console versions bring the same core gameplay experience, including the same aircraft, weather systems, and global map, while taking advantage of the hardware's power for smooth, console-friendly gameplay.

- **Cloud Gaming**: Thanks to Xbox Cloud Gaming (part of Xbox Game Pass), players can even stream the game on Xbox consoles or mobile devices without needing to own high-end hardware. This means you can fly anytime, anywhere, as long as you have a reliable internet connection.

Beyond the Platforms:

- For those looking to dive into VR, *Microsoft Flight Simulator 2024* offers full support for VR headsets, such as the Oculus Rift and HTC Vive. The VR experience brings an unparalleled sense of immersion, allowing players to step into the cockpit as if they were actually flying. With new updates to improve VR compatibility and performance, the game supports even the most demanding VR setups for a truly cinematic flying experience.

- **Third-Party Support**: As with previous versions of the game, MSFS 2024 also offers robust support for third-party modding, with a large and active community creating custom aircraft, scenery packs, and additional missions.

Chapter 1

New Horizons: What's New in MSFS 2024?

Microsoft Flight Simulator 2024 continues to raise the bar for flight simulation, offering fresh innovations, new features, and improvements that expand the depth of the game. Whether you're a seasoned pilot or a newcomer, *MSFS 2024* delivers an even more immersive, dynamic, and lifelike flying experience. From entirely new aircraft to dramatic enhancements in the game's maps and graphics, *MSFS 2024* pushes the limits of virtual aviation.

This section dives into all the exciting new features that set *MSFS 2024* apart from its predecessors, including the arrival of new aircraft, updates to the global maps, groundbreaking technical innovations, and major upgrades to real-world data and graphics that make every flight feel like a true adventure.

New Aircraft, Maps, and Technical Innovations

New Aircraft for Every Pilot

MSFS 2024 introduces a slew of new aircraft across various categories, offering something for every type of pilot. From small, agile planes to massive airliners, there are new flying machines that will excite both new and veteran players. The game focuses on expanding its fleet with detailed, realistic flight models and advanced systems to challenge even the most experienced pilots.

- **Iconic Commercial Airliners**:
  - Among the major additions in *MSFS 2024* is a new batch of commercial airliners, with updates to existing aircraft like the **Boeing 787 Dreamliner** and the **Airbus A320**, both of which have received more detailed cockpit systems and better navigation setups. But the real star is the **Boeing 777X**, a long-haul, ultra-modern aircraft that comes with a stunningly detailed flight deck and cutting-edge systems for a realistic flying experience.

- **General Aviation Aircraft**:
  - The general aviation segment also receives several new models, including the **Piper Aerostar 600** and the **Beechcraft King Air 350i**. These planes are perfect for players looking to explore more scenic routes or enjoy challenging flights in smaller, more nimble aircraft.

- **Experimental and Vintage Aircraft**:
  - *MSFS 2024* introduces several experimental aircraft, including the **P-51**

Mustang, a classic World War II-era fighter, and the **Lockheed Martin F-22 Raptor**. These high-speed, maneuverable aircraft offer a radically different flying experience and allow players to test their skills with advanced combat flight mechanics.

Expanded Maps: Explore the World in Detail

One of the standout features of *Microsoft Flight Simulator* has always been the stunning global map. With *MSFS 2024*, this map has been expanded and refined, offering even greater fidelity in the game's topographical and environmental data. The map now covers more areas in greater detail, offering an unprecedented flying experience.

- **Enhanced Photogrammetry**:
    - The game's photogrammetry technology, which converts real-world imagery into highly detailed 3D models of the environment, has received a significant update. Cities, rural areas, mountains, and coastlines are now more accurate, allowing for stunning aerial views and a truly lifelike representation of the globe.
- **Expanded Global Coverage**:

- o New regions have been added to the game, including more in-depth coverage of remote areas like the **Amazon Rainforest**, **Antarctica**, and **Sub-Saharan Africa**. These updates are perfect for players looking to take their flights off the beaten path and explore areas not previously well-covered.

- **Improved Terrain and Water Simulation**:
    - o Terrain and water simulation have been upgraded for *MSFS 2024*. Water bodies now feature more realistic effects like waves, currents, and reflections that change dynamically with the time of day and weather conditions. The terrain is more accurately rendered, with enhanced mountain ranges, valleys, and forests, offering an even more immersive experience as you soar across the globe.

- **Dynamic Terrain and Urban Growth**:
    - o As cities grow and change in the real world, *MSFS 2024* updates its urban landscapes to reflect these changes. Real-time data integration means that players can fly over ever-evolving metropolitan areas, witnessing new infrastructure, skylines, and landmarks in action.

Technical Innovations That Push the Limits

The technical innovations in *MSFS 2024* set a new standard for the flight simulation genre. These advancements offer better performance, more realistic systems, and increased immersion.

- **Real-Time Global Weather System**:
    - Building on its predecessor, *MSFS 2024* introduces an even more dynamic real-time weather system that takes into account everything from jet streams to atmospheric pressure. Players can encounter unpredictable weather patterns that influence flight performance in ways never seen before. This includes **real-time storms**, **snowfall**, and **turbulence**, which are generated using live weather data.

- **Advanced Flight Modeling**:
    - The flight models for each aircraft are more detailed, with true-to-life responses to a range of environmental factors such as wind gusts, air pressure, and temperature. These improvements make every flight feel distinct and real, as aircraft now respond more precisely to changes in atmospheric conditions, making flying feel even more challenging.

- **AI-Powered Traffic and Airspace**:
    - The AI systems for air traffic have been significantly improved, with more

accurate and dynamic flight paths for both commercial airliners and general aviation aircraft. The AI now better simulates air traffic congestion, holding patterns, and flight scheduling, allowing players to feel like they are part of a bustling, living airspace.

- **Virtual Reality (VR) Enhancements:**
  - *MSFS 2024* includes further enhancements to its VR functionality, providing players with a truly immersive experience. The cockpit's layout, instrument feedback, and world interactions are now fully optimized for VR, making flying feel like an entirely new reality. With VR support, you can look around the cockpit, interact with switches, and fly through dynamic weather systems, all from a fully immersive point of view.

Updated Real-World Data and Graphics Enhancements

One of the most impressive advancements in *Microsoft Flight Simulator 2024* is the integration of real-world data and groundbreaking graphics improvements. These updates allow players to experience a level of realism previously unimaginable in the genre.

Real-Time Satellite Data for Greater Accuracy

The game continues to use satellite and aerial imagery to capture the world's geography in the highest possible detail. In *MSFS 2024*, this data is even more accurate and up-to-date, ensuring that the world you fly over is as close to reality as possible.

- **Upgraded Satellite Imaging**:
    - The satellite images used in the game have been improved to provide higher-resolution textures and better detail for both urban and rural environments. You'll notice greater detail in landscapes, with individual buildings, roads, and trees rendered more realistically than ever before.

- **Weather Data Integration**:
    - The real-time weather feature in *MSFS 2024* has been enhanced with better integration of meteorological data. Players now experience weather patterns that align more closely with actual conditions, from precise cloud movements to accurate air pressure readings. This allows for more challenging and dynamic flight conditions.

Photorealistic Graphics Engine Enhancements

The graphics engine in *MSFS 2024* has undergone a significant overhaul, providing sharper, more lifelike visuals that take full advantage of modern hardware.

- **Improved Lighting and Shadow Systems**:
    - The lighting and shadow systems have been improved for a more natural and immersive experience. Sunsets, sunrises, and nighttime flights are more atmospheric than ever, with realistic lighting reflecting off clouds, water, and surfaces. The dynamic lighting system creates beautiful, accurate visual effects based on the time of day and weather conditions.

- **More Realistic Water and Terrain Effects**:
    - Water effects, such as reflections, ripples, and dynamic tides, have been enhanced, making ocean and lake flights more realistic. Additionally, terrain features like mountain ranges, valleys, and deserts have been upgraded with more detailed texturing, improving the overall feel of every flight.

- **Higher-Resolution 3D Models**:
    - Every aircraft, building, and landscape feature in *MSFS 2024* has been modeled in greater detail, with higher polygon counts and realistic textures. This ensures that every flight feels more grounded and lifelike, whether you're flying over a bustling city or a remote island.

Gameplay Essentials

Getting Started: Your First Flight

Embarking on your first flight in *Microsoft Flight Simulator 2024* is an exciting adventure. The game offers a rich experience, but if you're new to flight simulators, it's important to take it one step at a time. This section will guide you through the essential steps to ensure you're prepared to soar through the skies with confidence.

Step 1: Selecting Your Aircraft

The first decision you'll make as a new pilot is which aircraft to fly. *Microsoft Flight Simulator 2024* includes a wide variety of aircraft, ranging from small general aviation planes to large commercial airliners. For your first flight, it's recommended to start with a smaller, more forgiving aircraft. Here are a few options that will help you get a feel for basic flight:

- **Cessna 172 Skyhawk**: This is the perfect beginner aircraft. It's a light single-engine plane with easy handling and stable flight dynamics. It's used for training in the real world and provides a straightforward introduction to flight controls.
- **Piper Cub J-3**: Another great choice for beginners, the Piper Cub is a tailwheel aircraft with simple controls and a slow, steady flight

path. It's ideal for practicing takeoffs, landings, and basic navigation.

- **Airbus A320**: If you're feeling adventurous and want to jump into something larger, the Airbus A320 offers an easier entry into commercial flight with an automated cockpit system. It's an excellent introduction to modern jetliners for those who wish to explore advanced systems later on.

Once you've selected your aircraft, you're ready to move on to the next step: setting up your flight.

Step 2: Choosing Your Flight Plan

Before you take off, you'll need to set your flight plan. *Microsoft Flight Simulator 2024* includes several easy-to-use tools to help with this. For beginners, you can start with a short, simple flight.

1. **Starting Location**: Select an airport to start your flight. Beginners should choose smaller, less complex airports with straightforward runways. Well-known beginner-friendly airports like **Los Angeles International (LAX)** or **San Francisco International (SFO)** are good places to start.

2. **Flight Path**: If you're unfamiliar with planning a flight, you can use the game's default flight plans, which will take you on scenic routes around the world. If you want to make things simple, choose a flight that stays within a manageable area,

avoiding complicated routes with airways and multiple waypoints.

3. **Weather and Time**: As a beginner, you'll want to start with calm weather conditions—clear skies and light winds. You can adjust the time of day based on your preference, but a daytime flight offers the best visibility for learning. You can gradually increase the complexity of weather conditions as you become more experienced.

Step 3: Familiarizing Yourself with the Cockpit

Once your flight plan is set, it's time to familiarize yourself with the aircraft's cockpit. Every aircraft in *MSFS 2024* has a different layout, but all of them share some common instruments:

- **Primary Flight Display (PFD)**: Shows critical flight information like altitude, airspeed, heading, and flight attitude. This is your primary instrument for flying.

- **Throttle and Engine Controls**: These control the engine's power output. The throttle lever adjusts the speed of your plane.

- **Control Yoke or Joystick**: This is your primary tool for controlling the aircraft's pitch (up and down), roll (left and right), and yaw (turning left or right).

As a beginner, it's a good idea to start by simply familiarizing yourself with the layout and understanding where these basic controls are located.

Step 4: Taking Off

- **Start the Engine**: In *MSFS 2024*, starting your aircraft can be either automatic or manual, depending on the aircraft. For smaller aircraft, you'll need to engage the starter and monitor your engine gauges to ensure everything is functioning properly.

- **Taxiing to the Runway**: Use the throttle and rudder (or pedals, if available) to move your aircraft from the parking area to the runway. Make sure to follow the taxiway lines as you head toward the runway.

- **Takeoff**: Once you've aligned with the runway, increase the throttle gradually. In the Cessna 172, you'll need to apply back pressure to the control yoke to lift the nose and initiate your climb. Keep your speed and altitude steady, and use small inputs on the yoke to maintain a smooth climb.

Step 5: Flying and Navigating

- **Maintaining Altitude**: As you reach your cruising altitude, maintain a steady climb and ensure your airspeed is within safe limits. Use the autopilot system in advanced aircraft like the Airbus A320 to help you with altitude hold and heading control.

- **Turning and Navigation**: Use the plane's heading indicator to turn the aircraft as needed. To navigate from one point to another, you can either fly visually (VFR) or rely on the aircraft's GPS system for more precise direction (IFR).

Step 6: Landing

Landing is one of the most challenging aspects of flying. But don't worry; with practice, you'll master the art of approach and landing.

- **Approach**: As you approach your destination airport, reduce your altitude and speed gradually. Ensure your approach is lined up with the runway. In smaller aircraft, this is done manually, while larger aircraft often use autopilot for approach.

- **Final Approach and Touchdown**: On final approach, align the aircraft with the runway and begin to lower the landing gear (if applicable). Gradually decrease throttle as you approach the runway, and apply small adjustments to your pitch and roll. As you reach the runway, pull back gently on the yoke or stick to flare the aircraft and soften the landing.

Step 7: Taxiing to Parking

After you've successfully landed, taxi off the runway and follow the signs to the parking area. Shut down the engines, and your first flight in *Microsoft Flight Simulator 2024* is complete!

Quick Start Guide for New Pilots

For new pilots looking for a quick overview before diving in, here's a simplified guide to getting started:

1. **Select Your Aircraft**: Choose a beginner-friendly plane like the Cessna 172.

2. **Pick a Simple Flight Plan**: Start with a short, calm-weather flight from one airport to another.

3. **Learn Basic Controls**: Familiarize yourself with the throttle, yoke, and basic instruments.

4. **Takeoff and Flying**: Use the throttle to take off, maintain a steady altitude, and explore.

5. **Practice Landing**: Approach your destination runway, reduce speed, and practice your landing.

Don't worry if things don't go perfectly on your first flight—take it slow, and with practice, you'll gain confidence and skill.

Game Installation and Setup

Before you can begin your aviation adventure, you'll need to install *Microsoft Flight Simulator 2024* and get everything set up. Here's a step-by-step guide to help you get started.

Step 1: Installing the Game

1. **Download**: If you purchased *Microsoft Flight Simulator 2024* through the Microsoft Store, Steam, or Xbox Game Pass, navigate to your

chosen platform and begin downloading the game. Depending on your internet speed and the platform, this can take some time, as the game requires a substantial amount of data for its stunning visuals and world-building.

2. **System Requirements**: Before installing, ensure your computer meets the minimum or recommended system requirements. These include:

    - **Operating System**: Windows 10 or later (64-bit)
    - **Processor**: Intel i5-8400 / AMD Ryzen 5 1500X or better
    - **Graphics**: NVIDIA GTX 1060 / AMD Radeon RX 580 or better
    - **Memory**: 16GB RAM or more
    - **Storage**: SSD with at least 150GB of free space

3. **Install**: Once downloaded, follow the on-screen instructions to install the game on your system. If you're installing via a physical copy, insert the disk and follow the installation prompts.

Step 2: Setting Up Your Hardware

- **Controllers**: You can play with a joystick, flight yoke, pedals, or a simple gamepad, but for the best experience, a flight joystick or yoke is recommended. For new players, a basic joystick like the **Logitech Extreme 3D Pro** is a great choice to start.

- **Flight Yoke Setup**: If you're using a flight yoke, connect it to your computer via USB, and then calibrate it in the game's settings menu to ensure smooth control of the aircraft.

- **Rudder Pedals**: Rudder pedals are optional but enhance realism, allowing for better control of the aircraft's yaw during takeoff, landing, and in-flight maneuvers.

Step 3: Configuring Settings

- **Graphics Settings**: *MSFS 2024* is a graphically intensive game, so adjust your settings based on your hardware. If you have a high-end PC, you can enable the highest graphical settings for ultra-realistic visuals. For lower-end systems, you may need to lower settings for smoother performance.

- **Control Settings**: In the options menu, customize the keybindings or joystick/yoke inputs to your liking. You can also adjust sensitivity and dead zones to match your preference.

Step 4: Updates and Patches

- **Automatic Updates**: *Microsoft Flight Simulator* regularly receives updates to improve gameplay, fix bugs, and enhance content. Ensure your game is set to auto-update, so you always have the latest features and improvements.

Now that your game is set up, you're ready to begin your journey as a virtual pilot. Take off into the skies, explore new horizons, and enjoy everything *Microsoft Flight Simulator 2024* has to offer! Let me know if you'd like to expand any sections or dive deeper into other gameplay aspects!

Chapter 2

Mastering the Controls

Whether you're a beginner or an advanced pilot, mastering the controls is essential to getting the most out of *Microsoft Flight Simulator 2024*. The game offers a variety of control schemes to suit your experience level and hardware setup. In this section, we'll break down the basic controls for new pilots, discuss advanced settings for more experienced sim enthusiasts, and help you choose the right flight setup.

Basic Controls for Beginners

As a beginner, understanding the basic flight controls will help you gain confidence in the cockpit. *Microsoft Flight Simulator 2024* offers a realistic experience, but the fundamentals remain relatively simple.

1. Throttle

- **Throttle Control**: The throttle controls the engine power and, by extension, the speed of your aircraft. On a joystick or yoke, the throttle is typically represented as a slider or a rotary knob.
    - o **Increase Throttle**: Move the throttle forward to increase engine power and accelerate.

- **Decrease Throttle**: Move the throttle backward to reduce power and slow down.

Beginners should focus on smooth throttle management. A steady increase in throttle will help with a stable takeoff, and careful reduction will allow for a gentle descent and landing.

2. Elevator (Pitch Control)

- **Control Stick or Yoke**: The elevator controls the aircraft's pitch, or how the plane moves up and down (nose up or nose down). Moving the joystick or yoke forward lowers the nose, while pulling it back raises the nose.
    - **To Climb**: Gently pull the yoke or joystick back to raise the aircraft's nose.
    - **To Descend**: Push the yoke or joystick forward to lower the nose and initiate a descent.

At the beginning of your flight, you'll want to maintain a slight climb rate after takeoff by gently pulling back on the control.

3. Ailerons (Roll Control)

- **Control Stick or Yoke**: The ailerons control the aircraft's roll, causing it to bank left or right. To bank left, push the control stick to the left, and to bank right, push the control stick to the right.

- **Left Bank**: Push the left side of the joystick or yoke to the left.
- **Right Bank**: Push the right side of the joystick or yoke to the right.

Bank controls are essential when navigating turns. Beginners should practice gentle turns to avoid overbanking, especially in smaller aircraft.

4. Rudder (Yaw Control)

- **Rudder Pedals or Joystick Twist**: The rudder controls the yaw of the aircraft, which is the left or right movement of the nose. It helps you stay coordinated during turns and counteract forces from crosswinds.
  - **To Turn Left**: Push the left rudder pedal or twist the joystick left.
  - **To Turn Right**: Push the right rudder pedal or twist the joystick right.

Use the rudder in conjunction with ailerons during turns to maintain smooth flight. It's especially important in crosswind landings or when performing tight maneuvers.

5. Flaps

- **Flap Control**: Flaps are used to increase lift at lower speeds and are especially useful during takeoff and landing. You can control flaps through a button or a slider, depending on your setup.

- **Takeoff**: Set your flaps to about 10-15% for takeoff to ensure smoother lift-off.
- **Landing**: Increase flaps to around 30-40% for a slower approach and shorter landing distance.

6. Trim

- **Trim Control**: Trim helps adjust the aircraft's pitch to relieve control pressure. This is especially helpful during long flights, as it reduces the need for constant control inputs.
    - **Trim for Climb**: If the aircraft's nose tends to dip during a climb, use the trim to raise the nose without adjusting the elevator.
    - **Trim for Level Flight**: Adjust the trim to maintain level flight when you've reached cruising altitude.

As a beginner, focus on using the trim to keep the aircraft level and reduce unnecessary strain on the joystick or yoke.

Advanced Settings for Sim Pilots

For more experienced pilots, *Microsoft Flight Simulator 2024* provides a range of advanced settings to fine-tune your flying experience and take full control over your aircraft.

1. Sensitivity Settings

- **Control Sensitivity**: In the options menu, you can adjust the sensitivity of your joystick or yoke. This affects how quickly the aircraft responds to your control inputs. For advanced users, setting the sensitivity to a more responsive level can give you a more precise feel.
    - **Low Sensitivity**: Provides smooth, less aggressive responses, which can help avoid overcorrection, especially for beginners.
    - **High Sensitivity**: Results in more immediate, sharper responses. This is suitable for more experienced pilots who want to make precise adjustments.

2. Dead Zones

- **Dead Zone Adjustments**: The dead zone is the area around the center of the control stick where no input is registered. Reducing the dead zone can make your control inputs more responsive.
    - **Smaller Dead Zones**: If you prefer high precision, reduce the dead zone so that the aircraft reacts immediately to small joystick or yoke movements.
    - **Larger Dead Zones**: If you want a more forgiving control response, increase the dead zone to prevent accidental movements.

3. **Autopilot Settings**

- **Autopilot Mode**: *MSFS 2024* allows you to set autopilot for altitude, heading, and navigation. Experienced pilots can fine-tune the autopilot to manage complex flight plans.
    - **Altitude Hold**: Use this to maintain a constant altitude during long flights.
    - **Heading Hold**: This keeps the aircraft on a straight path, useful for cruising.
    - **LNAV/VNAV**: For flight planning and automation, you can set the aircraft to follow a route via waypoints (LNAV) and automatically adjust your altitude based on flight plans (VNAV).

4. **Advanced Instrumentation**

- **Glass Cockpits**: Modern aircraft in *MSFS 2024* often feature digital "glass cockpits" that provide flight information through multifunction displays (MFDs). Sim pilots can interact with the cockpit displays and customize them for specific needs, such as navigating via GPS, adjusting radio frequencies, and monitoring engine parameters.

- **Custom Instrument Panels**: For more precise control, some aircraft in *MSFS 2024* let you choose between different flight display layouts. You can add or remove various instruments, such as altitude indicators, artificial horizons, or navigation systems.

Choosing Your Flight Setup: Joystick, Controller, or Keyboard

Choosing the right setup for your flight experience depends on your personal preferences and level of commitment to flight simulation. Below are the advantages and considerations for different control setups:

1. Joystick Setup

A joystick is the most common and affordable option for sim pilots who want a more immersive experience. It's ideal for general aviation aircraft and gives you intuitive control over the aircraft's roll, pitch, and yaw.

- **Best For**: General aviation aircraft, beginners, and casual players.
- **Pros**: Compact, inexpensive, easy to set up, and sufficient for most flight types.
- **Cons**: Limited control for more complex aircraft or long-distance flying.

2. Flight Yoke and Pedals Setup

For a more immersive and professional experience, a flight yoke combined with rudder pedals is the gold standard for flight simulation. This setup offers greater precision for controlling aircraft, especially during takeoffs, landings, and general flying.

- **Best For**: Serious flight sim enthusiasts, long-haul flights, and commercial aircraft.

- **Pros**: Precise control, more realistic flying experience, comfortable for long flights, and best suited for aircraft with traditional yokes (e.g., Cessna 172, Airbus A320).

- **Cons**: Expensive, takes up more space, and requires a larger setup.

3. Controller Setup (Gamepad)

Using a controller, such as an Xbox controller or a gamepad, is a more casual option. While it doesn't offer the level of precision that a joystick or yoke setup provides, it's still functional for beginners and players who prefer a more accessible, all-in-one solution.

- **Best For**: Casual players, those who want a quick start without much investment, or for shorter, simpler flights.

- **Pros**: Affordable, easy to use, portable, and doesn't require additional peripherals.

- **Cons**: Limited precision and realism, especially for more advanced aircraft.

4. Keyboard and Mouse Setup

While not ideal for realistic flight simulation, using a keyboard and mouse is possible for beginners who just want to get started without additional peripherals.

However, this is the least immersive method and is typically only suitable for very basic flights.

- **Best For**: Extremely casual players, those testing the game without investing in peripherals.
- **Pros**: No need for additional hardware, easy for light exploration.
- **Cons**: Lack of precision, poor control for complex flight maneuvers, and no feedback from the aircraft.

Chapter 3

Camera & View Modes: Finding Your Perfect View

In *Microsoft Flight Simulator 2024*, the camera system plays a crucial role in your flying experience. Whether you prefer the immersive view from within the cockpit, the expansive view of your aircraft from the exterior, or a more flexible perspective with the drone camera, *MSFS 2024* offers various camera modes to cater to different flight styles and preferences.

This section will help you navigate through the different camera options and show you how to customize camera angles for better control and comfort during your flights.

Cockpit, Exterior, and Drone Camera Options

1. Cockpit Camera (Most Immersive View)

The **Cockpit Camera** is the most immersive and realistic view in *Microsoft Flight Simulator 2024*, as it places you directly in the pilot's seat. This view provides an accurate representation of the aircraft's interior, giving you access to all the controls, instruments, and systems as they would appear in real life.

- **Advantages**:
  - **Realism**: Experience the true feeling of being a pilot as you interact with the cockpit's controls and gauges.
  - **Instrument Readouts**: Provides direct access to all instruments, which is essential for navigation, monitoring engine performance, and autopilot settings.
  - **Interaction**: You can manipulate switches, knobs, and levers in the cockpit (depending on the aircraft model), adding an additional layer of realism.
- **Key Controls**:
  - **Look Around**: Use the mouse or a joystick to look around the cockpit. Right-click and drag to look at specific instruments or switch panels.
  - **Zoom**: Use the mouse scroll wheel or assigned controls to zoom in or out for a closer or wider view of the cockpit instruments.
- **Best For**: Pilots who want the most realistic and immersive experience, especially those focusing on managing the aircraft systems or engaging in IFR (Instrument Flight Rules) navigation.

2. Exterior Camera (Wide-Angle Aircraft View)

The **Exterior Camera** allows you to view the aircraft from the outside, giving you a bird's-eye view of the plane and the environment around it. This view is essential for seeing the aircraft's movement relative to the world and can be used for cinematic shots, inspection views, or simply for a different perspective during flight.

- **Advantages**:
    - **Situational Awareness**: Offers a full view of your aircraft's position, allowing you to monitor flight maneuvers, turns, and speed in relation to the terrain and surrounding areas.
    - **Aesthetic View**: Great for taking screenshots or enjoying scenic flights, as it provides a wide-angle view of your surroundings and aircraft.
- **Key Controls**:
    - **Camera Toggle**: Switch between exterior views by pressing the relevant button or keybind (usually "End" or a custom shortcut).
    - **Angle Adjustments**: Move the camera around the aircraft by using the directional controls, or zoom in/out to adjust the camera distance.
- **Best For**: Players who want to appreciate the visual beauty of *MSFS 2024* or gain a better

understanding of the aircraft's flight path from the outside.

3. Drone Camera (Freeform Exploration)

The **Drone Camera** offers the most flexible and freeform perspective in the game. You can use the drone camera to fly anywhere around your aircraft or even travel across the entire world, exploring from the ground or above.

- **Advantages**:
    - **Unlimited Freedom**: Fly around your aircraft, zoom in to examine it closely, or even explore distant landmarks. The drone camera allows complete freedom of movement.
    - **Cinematic Shots**: Perfect for creating stunning aerial photography or cinematic videos. You can capture unique angles, such as flying above a mountain range or zooming through cityscapes.
    - **Precise Control**: Offers precise control over your movement, allowing for slow, calculated movements or faster, more dramatic camera sweeps.
- **Key Controls**:
    - **Camera Movement**: Use the WASD keys or a joystick to move the drone in all directions (up, down, left, right, forward,

and backward). You can also control the speed and direction of the drone's flight.

- o **Camera Rotation**: Use the mouse or joystick to rotate the camera freely and zoom in or out to adjust your perspective.

- **Best For**: Cinematic flights, exploring your aircraft in detail, or capturing screenshots and videos of breathtaking environments.

Customizing Camera Angles for Better Control

Customizing your camera angles is key to optimizing your flying experience, especially when it comes to navigating through complex airspace, landing in challenging conditions, or simply improving comfort while flying. *Microsoft Flight Simulator 2024* provides several options for adjusting and saving your preferred camera views.

1. Adjusting Cockpit View for Better Control

For better control in the cockpit view, you can adjust the seat position, angle, and zoom to ensure you're comfortable while managing the aircraft's controls.

- **Seat Position**:
    - o **Forward/Backward**: Adjust the seat position to give you a better view of the controls or the horizon.

pg. 46

- **Up/Down**: Move your seat up or down to align your view with the horizon or instruments, which is particularly useful for certain aircraft with unique cockpit designs.

- **Field of View (FOV)**:
    - **Adjust FOV**: Increase or decrease your field of view to capture more of the cockpit or focus on specific instruments. This is especially useful for larger aircraft with more complex cockpits or smaller aircraft where you may need to focus on a narrow area.

- **Tilt Angle**:
    - **Pitch Angle**: Adjust the camera's tilt to change the angle at which you view the cockpit instruments. This can be helpful in tight spaces or when flying at extreme altitudes.

2. Customizing Exterior and Drone Views

To capture the perfect angle while flying outside the aircraft, you can fine-tune your exterior and drone camera settings for better control over your surroundings.

- **Fixed Exterior Camera**:
    - For a fixed, non-moving camera that follows the aircraft from a certain distance,

set the camera angle at a fixed point and lock it in place. This is useful when you want to track the aircraft while it moves through a predetermined path.

- **Drone Camera Speed**:
    - **Speed Adjustment**: You can adjust the drone camera speed, which is perfect for smoother movement when you want a cinematic experience or faster speeds for quick exploration.

- **Freeform View with Hotkeys**:
    - Assign hotkeys for quick camera adjustments (such as resetting the camera view, switching between camera modes, or returning to a predefined angle). This can save time and make switching between views seamless.

3. Saving and Switching Between Custom Camera Angles

Once you've customized your camera settings, it's a good idea to save your preferred views so you can quickly switch between them during your flights. *MSFS 2024* allows you to save camera presets, so you can easily load your preferred view at any time during your session.

- **Creating Camera Presets**:
    - **Save View**: Once you've positioned your camera at your desired angle (cockpit,

exterior, or drone), you can save the view as a preset. This can be done through the camera settings menu.

- **Switching Views**:
    - You can cycle through your saved views quickly by pressing your assigned hotkeys for each preset. This allows you to move seamlessly from your cockpit view to an external view or drone view without having to manually adjust the camera.

4. Using TrackIR or Virtual Reality (VR)

For players with **TrackIR** or **VR setups**, you can integrate these technologies to further enhance your camera control. TrackIR allows you to move your head to look around the cockpit, while VR provides a fully immersive experience where you can look around naturally in all directions.

- **TrackIR**: Simply enable TrackIR in the camera settings, and you'll be able to move your head to control the viewpoint in the cockpit.

- **VR**: For full immersion, *MSFS 2024* fully supports VR. You can adjust the VR settings for better clarity, comfort, and positional control.

Best Camera Modes for Different Flight Scenarios

- **Landing and Approach**: Use the cockpit view to manage your instruments and autopilot settings, then switch to an exterior view for a clear perspective of the runway and your aircraft's alignment.

- **Long-Distance Flights**: Use the cockpit camera for managing systems and navigation, then switch to drone view for relaxation and sightseeing as you fly across vast landscapes.

- **Exploring New Terrain**: Use the drone camera to freely explore cities, mountains, or landmarks from any angle. It allows you to move at your own pace and zoom in for the best view.

Aircraft & Customization

In *Microsoft Flight Simulator 2024*, aircraft play a central role in your flying experience, and the game offers a diverse and expansive fleet. Whether you're flying a small, nimble single-engine plane or commanding a massive commercial airliner, each aircraft is meticulously modeled to offer a unique flying experience. In this section, we'll explore the wide variety of aircraft available in the game, provide an overview of their key features, and delve into the customization options available for each one.

All About Aircraft: Your Flying Machines

From small propeller-driven planes to large, complex jets, the aircraft in *Microsoft Flight Simulator 2024* are designed to be as realistic as possible, with every model reflecting the true performance, handling, and systems of their real-world counterparts. Each aircraft has been carefully crafted to provide both new and experienced pilots with the right level of challenge, realism, and fun.

Types of Aircraft in MSFS 2024:

- **General Aviation (GA)**: These small, single-engine planes are perfect for beginners and intermediate pilots. They are highly maneuverable, ideal for short flights, and often used for flight training.

- **Commercial Airliners**: These large, complex aircraft are designed for long-haul flights, carrying hundreds of passengers across continents. They require more advanced flight management systems and are suited for experienced sim pilots who want to tackle realistic airline operations.

- **Military and Special Aircraft**: *MSFS 2024* also includes high-performance military aircraft like fighter jets and bombers, offering an entirely different type of flying experience with fast speeds, sharp turns, and powerful engines.

- **Helicopters**: For those looking to experience vertical flight, helicopters in *MSFS 2024* provide an exciting and challenging flight model. Helicopter flying is quite different from fixed-wing aircraft and offers its own set of challenges and rewards.

- **Exotic and Experimental Aircraft**: The game includes experimental planes and unconventional aircraft that are not typically seen in traditional simulators, allowing for truly unique flying experiences.

Key Features of MSFS 2024 Aircraft:

- **Realistic Flight Dynamics**: Each aircraft in *MSFS 2024* behaves according to its real-world flight characteristics. Whether you're flying a small Cessna 172 or a massive Boeing 747, the way the aircraft responds to control inputs, weather conditions, and flight maneuvers is true to life.

- **Detailed Cockpits**: Aircraft in *MSFS 2024* come with fully functional and highly detailed cockpits. From analog dials to advanced glass cockpits, every switch, lever, and button is interactive, allowing players to operate their aircraft like real pilots.

- **Engine and System Management**: Aircraft in *MSFS 2024* feature realistic engine performance and system management. From checking fuel levels to managing electrical systems, understanding and controlling an aircraft's systems is key to a successful flight.

- **Autopilot and Navigation Systems**: Many aircraft feature advanced autopilot and navigation systems. From simple heading hold in small aircraft to full flight management systems in commercial airliners, learning to use these systems can help reduce workload and improve flight accuracy.

Overview of Aircraft Available in MSFS 2024

Microsoft Flight Simulator 2024 offers an incredibly broad selection of aircraft. Below, we'll provide an overview of the types of aircraft you can fly in the game, ranging from small planes perfect for casual flights to complex commercial airliners requiring advanced piloting skills.

General Aviation (GA) Aircraft

General aviation aircraft are among the most accessible in the game, offering easy handling and a great introduction to flying. These planes are designed for short trips, offering a close-up view of the world below and giving pilots a true feel for how small aircraft handle.

- **Cessna 172 Skyhawk**: One of the most iconic training aircraft, the Cessna 172 is perfect for beginners. It's easy to fly, offers stable handling, and comes with basic avionics, making it a great starting point for new pilots.

- **Piper Cub J-3**: A classic taildragger with a simple, rugged design, the Piper Cub is ideal for exploring rural landscapes and practicing fundamental flying techniques. It's slow and stable, perfect for learning how to control an aircraft without overwhelming the pilot.

- **Beechcraft Bonanza**: A step up from basic GA planes, the Bonanza is a fast, four-seater with excellent performance. With more advanced avionics, it's suited for intermediate pilots looking to expand their skills.

- **Cirrus SR22**: A modern, high-performance aircraft, the Cirrus SR22 is equipped with advanced avionics and features a sleek design. It's perfect for those looking to tackle more complex systems while still enjoying the speed and flexibility of a GA aircraft.

Commercial Airliners

For more experienced pilots, *MSFS 2024* offers a wide selection of commercial airliners. These aircraft are designed to simulate long-haul flights, complete with advanced autopilot systems, detailed flight management, and real-world navigation.

- **Airbus A320neo**: A modern and widely used airliner, the A320neo features advanced fly-by-wire systems and a glass cockpit. It's an ideal choice for those looking to experience the intricacies of commercial flight, from cruising altitudes to precision landings.

- **Boeing 787 Dreamliner**: The Dreamliner is one of the most advanced aircraft in the world, designed for long-haul flights. With cutting-edge technology and high-efficiency engines, flying the 787 is a challenging but rewarding experience.

Players will need to master the aircraft's avionics, autopilot systems, and fuel management.

- **Boeing 747-8**: Known as the "Queen of the Skies," the 747 is a legendary airliner with a distinct design. It's perfect for pilots who want to experience large aircraft and manage everything from autopilot settings to passenger comfort on long flights.

- **Airbus A330**: Another long-haul airliner, the A330 is known for its versatility and passenger capacity. It's a great choice for pilots interested in mastering advanced flight systems and operating one of the world's most popular wide-body airliners.

Military and Special Aircraft

MSFS 2024 also includes a variety of military and special purpose aircraft, offering a different flying experience that emphasizes speed, agility, and precision.

- **F/A-18 Hornet**: A supersonic fighter jet, the F/A-18 is fast, agile, and perfect for handling complex maneuvers. It's designed for high-speed flight and military operations, providing a completely different experience compared to commercial airliners.

- **P-51 Mustang**: A World War II-era fighter plane, the P-51 Mustang is known for its speed and agility. Flying this iconic aircraft requires precision and skill, making it ideal for experienced players looking for a challenge.

- **Lockheed Martin F-22 Raptor**: A fifth-generation fighter jet with unmatched speed and maneuverability, the F-22 Raptor offers a dynamic flying experience. It's designed for players who want to push the limits of aerial performance.

Helicopters

Helicopters provide a completely different flying experience. They offer the ability to take off and land vertically, and their flight dynamics are unlike any fixed-wing aircraft.

- **Bell 407**: A popular civilian helicopter, the Bell 407 offers an excellent introduction to rotorcraft flying. It's perfect for players interested in exploring terrain that traditional aircraft cannot access.

- **Hughes 500**: A small, fast helicopter, the Hughes 500 is designed for agile maneuvers. It's a great choice for players who want to experience precision flying in tight spaces, such as search-and-rescue missions or flying through mountainous regions.

Exotic and Experimental Aircraft

For those looking to push the boundaries of aviation, *MSFS 2024* includes a variety of exotic and experimental aircraft that break away from traditional designs.

- **Concorde**: The supersonic passenger airliner is back, offering players the chance to experience the thrill of flying faster than the speed of sound. Flying the Concorde requires precise management of speed, altitude, and aerodynamics.
- **Vans RV-7**: A homebuilt aircraft, the RV-7 offers a fun and agile flying experience. It's fast, easy to control, and perfect for flying low and fast over scenic terrain.

Customization Options for Your Aircraft

Microsoft Flight Simulator 2024 also offers a variety of customization options for each aircraft, allowing players to personalize their flying machines and make them uniquely theirs.

1. Livery Customization

You can customize the aircraft's exterior with various liveries, ranging from default paint schemes to unique designs or even custom-made liveries. Players can download custom liveries from the in-game marketplace or create their own using third-party tools.

2. Performance and Systems Customization

Advanced users can tweak the aircraft's systems, including engine performance, fuel load, and weight distribution. For example:

- **Engine Settings**: Modify engine parameters for more realistic flight simulation.
- **Weight and Balance**: Adjust the aircraft's load to see how different configurations affect performance.

3. Cockpit Layout and Instrument Panels

In some aircraft, players can customize the cockpit layout, choosing which instruments are displayed and how they're arranged on the flight panel. This customization can improve visibility and flight efficiency.

4. Modding and Third-Party Aircraft

MSFS 2024 supports third-party mods, meaning you can download additional aircraft or custom mods that provide new flying machines with unique flight models or visual effects. The community has a wide variety of aircraft to choose from, ranging from vintage warbirds to futuristic spacecraft.

Chapter 4

Personalizing Your Aircraft

One of the most exciting features of *Microsoft Flight Simulator 2024* is the ability to personalize your aircraft, making it uniquely yours. Whether you're looking to add a custom livery, modify your aircraft's performance, or fine-tune its systems, *MSFS 2024* offers a variety of ways to customize your flying machine for both aesthetic appeal and optimal flight performance.

Livery Customization and Modding Options

1. Livery Customization: Painting Your Plane

Livery customization allows you to change the appearance of your aircraft by applying different paint schemes. This can range from classic airline liveries to personalized designs that reflect your own unique style. Whether you're flying a small Cessna or a massive airliner, custom liveries add a layer of personalization to your aircraft.

- **In-Game Livery Options**:
    - *MSFS 2024* comes with a selection of pre-installed liveries for a wide range of aircraft, from commercial airliners to

general aviation planes. These liveries are designed to reflect the real-world paint schemes of various airlines, companies, and private owners.

- **Creating Custom Liveries**:
    - For those who want something truly unique, *MSFS 2024* supports the creation and installation of custom liveries. You can either download liveries from the in-game marketplace or create your own using third-party software.
    - **Tools for Creating Liveries**: Programs like Photoshop or GIMP can be used to create liveries, using template files that match the aircraft's model. Once your livery is complete, you can install it into the game and select it in the aircraft's customization menu.
    - **Modding Communities**: The MSFS community has a vibrant modding scene, where users share their custom liveries. Websites like **Flightsim.to** and **MSFSAddon.com** are great places to find free and paid liveries for download.
- **Livery Installation**: After downloading or creating a custom livery, you'll need to install it into the *MSFS 2024* directory:

- Navigate to your **Community Folder** in *MSFS 2024* and paste the livery file.
- Once installed, the livery will appear in the aircraft customization menu, where you can select it just like any other paint scheme.

- **Customizing Aircraft Logos and Text**:
  - Many liveries can be further personalized with logos, text, or even custom decals. This is a fun way to represent your airline or personal brand. You can edit texture files directly to add logos or other images.

2. Modding Options for Aircraft

Modding allows players to enhance or completely change the design and behavior of aircraft in *MSFS 2024*. Whether you're adding new planes, changing how they handle, or enhancing their textures, modding opens up a whole new world of possibilities.

- **New Aircraft Models**:
  - The game supports the importation of third-party aircraft models created by independent developers. These models range from iconic vintage planes to futuristic aircraft, offering an entirely new flying experience.
  - Popular modding sites like **Flightsim.to** and **simMarket** offer a variety of aircraft

mods that can be downloaded and installed into the game.

- **Changing Aircraft Systems**:
    o Mods also allow for more complex customization, including tweaks to flight dynamics, engine performance, avionics, and autopilot systems. For example, if you prefer an aircraft with more challenging handling, you can adjust the aircraft's flight model to make it behave more realistically or add more depth to the cockpit systems.

- **Custom Sound Packs**:
    o Modding isn't limited to just visual elements; you can also change the sound environment of your aircraft. Custom sound packs can alter engine sounds, cockpit noises, and the atmospheric sounds you hear while flying, making your flight even more immersive.

Adjusting Systems and Configurations for Optimal Performance

While aesthetic customization is a great way to make your aircraft unique, adjusting systems and configurations to optimize performance is crucial for making sure your aircraft runs at its best. Whether you're looking to improve efficiency, flight characteristics, or handling, *MSFS 2024* offers several ways to tweak your aircraft's settings for optimal performance.

1. Engine Performance Tuning

Engine tuning allows you to adjust how your aircraft's engines respond to control inputs, how much power they produce, and how efficiently they burn fuel.

- **Engine Power Settings**: For larger aircraft, such as commercial jets, you can fine-tune the engine thrust and fuel consumption based on your flying needs. For example:
    - **Cruise Power**: Adjust the throttle for more efficient fuel usage during long-haul flights.
    - **Takeoff Thrust**: Set maximum power output for a smooth and powerful takeoff.
- **Fuel Efficiency Modifications**:
    - Some aircraft mods offer options to adjust fuel efficiency, allowing you to get the most out of your fuel load. This is particularly useful for long-haul flights, where optimizing fuel can make the difference in range and performance.
- **Overclocking Engines (Advanced)**:
    - For more experienced pilots, some mods allow you to overclock engine performance, increasing the engine's

power beyond standard settings. However, this comes at a cost, as it can affect the aircraft's handling and stress on the engine over time.

2. Flight Dynamics and Handling

Each aircraft in *MSFS 2024* behaves according to its specific flight model, and these dynamics can be adjusted for a more personalized experience.

- **Adjusting Control Surfaces**:
    - Tuning the control surfaces (elevator, ailerons, rudder) can change the responsiveness of the aircraft during flight. For example:
        - **Increased Sensitivity**: If you prefer a more responsive aircraft, increase the sensitivity of the control surfaces for quicker movements.
        - **Stabilization**: If you want smoother, more stable flight, you can reduce control sensitivity for a more relaxed flying experience.
- **Autopilot and Flight Management Systems**:
    - *MSFS 2024* allows for custom autopilot configurations. You can fine-tune the autopilot to better suit your needs,

adjusting how it handles altitude changes, speed control, and heading shifts.

- For advanced aircraft like the **Boeing 787** or **Airbus A320**, you can adjust the flight management systems (FMS) for more accurate route planning and automated handling.

- **Flight Model Modifications**:
  - Advanced users can tweak the aircraft's flight model to better reflect specific flight characteristics. This includes adjusting aerodynamic properties, stall speeds, and behavior during turbulence. Some aircraft mods available on third-party websites allow for in-depth adjustments to flight dynamics, providing a more customized flying experience.

3. Weight and Balance Adjustments

Weight and balance are essential components of aircraft performance, and *MSFS 2024* offers options to adjust these settings for each flight.

- **Fuel Load**: Adjusting the fuel load impacts your aircraft's weight and, consequently, its performance. A heavier aircraft will have longer takeoff distances, slower climb rates, and more sluggish handling. Lighter fuel loads improve maneuverability but reduce your range.

- **Passenger and Cargo Weight**: For aircraft that simulate real-world commercial airliners, you can adjust the amount of passengers and cargo, which will affect the total weight of the aircraft. Balancing the weight distribution across the aircraft is critical to maintaining stability and ensuring efficient flight.

- **Trim and Ballast**: Fine-tuning the trim settings or adding ballast can help you achieve optimal weight distribution, ensuring your aircraft handles smoothly, especially during takeoff and landing.

4. Avionics and Instrument Customization

Modern aircraft in *MSFS 2024* are equipped with complex avionics systems that offer a variety of customization options, allowing you to fine-tune your flight experience based on personal preferences.

- **Navigation Systems**: Modify the aircraft's GPS and navigation settings for more accurate flight planning, whether you're flying VFR (Visual Flight Rules) or IFR (Instrument Flight Rules). You can adjust waypoint displays, map zoom levels, and weather overlays to ensure the right level of information during your flight.

- **Cockpit Instrument Layout**: Some aircraft allow you to rearrange cockpit displays and panels. For instance, you can move the GPS unit, autopilot controls, or engine displays to more convenient locations based on your preferred flying style.

Flight Techniques & Tutorials

Whether you're a novice or an experienced pilot, mastering the essential flight techniques is crucial to your success in *Microsoft Flight Simulator 2024*. This section provides the fundamental techniques for flying, including takeoff, flying, and landing, as well as handling weather and environmental factors that can impact your flight. With these tutorials, you'll learn to fly like a pro and tackle a variety of flight conditions with confidence.

Flight School: Basics for Every Pilot

Before you take to the skies, it's essential to understand the basic principles of flight and how to operate an aircraft safely and efficiently. In this section, we'll break down the foundational elements of flight, from controls to flight dynamics, and provide beginner tips that every pilot should know.

1. Basic Flight Principles

To understand how to fly an aircraft, you need to grasp the basic forces at play during flight:

- **Lift**: The force that pushes the aircraft upwards, created by the wings as they interact with the air. The primary factor in lift is the speed of the aircraft and the angle of attack of the wings.
- **Thrust**: The force produced by the engines to propel the aircraft forward. The greater the

thrust, the faster the aircraft moves through the air.

- **Drag**: The resistance the aircraft experiences as it moves through the air. This can slow the plane down and needs to be overcome by sufficient thrust.

- **Weight**: The force pulling the aircraft down due to gravity. For an aircraft to become airborne, lift must exceed weight.

2. Key Flight Controls

- **Throttle**: Controls the engine power and dictates the aircraft's speed. To climb, you need to increase throttle; to descend, you reduce it.

- **Elevator (Pitch)**: This controls the aircraft's nose up or down. Pulling back on the control yoke or joystick raises the nose (climbs), while pushing it forward lowers the nose (descends).

- **Ailerons (Roll)**: Controls the aircraft's bank, or tilt, to the left or right. Moving the control yoke left or right causes the plane to roll in that direction.

- **Rudder (Yaw)**: Controls the aircraft's turning motion on its vertical axis. This is important during turns and when compensating for crosswinds.

3. Understanding the Flight Instruments

As a pilot, you need to understand and interpret the various flight instruments to ensure safe and efficient flying:

- **Airspeed Indicator**: Measures the aircraft's speed through the air. Ensure you stay within the safe operational speed for the aircraft.
- **Attitude Indicator**: Shows the orientation of the aircraft relative to the horizon. This is vital for maintaining control, especially when flying in poor visibility conditions.
- **Altitude Indicator**: Displays the aircraft's altitude, typically measured in feet above sea level.
- **Heading Indicator**: Shows the aircraft's current heading relative to the magnetic compass.
- **Vertical Speed Indicator**: Displays how quickly the aircraft is climbing or descending.

How to Take Off, Fly, and Land Like a Pro

Mastering takeoff, flight, and landing is essential to becoming a skilled pilot. These techniques form the backbone of every flight, whether you're taking a quick sightseeing tour or a long-haul journey.

1. Takeoff Procedures

- **Before Takeoff**:

- Ensure the aircraft's systems are configured properly (e.g., flaps, autopilot, trim).
- Check your instruments to verify engine performance, fuel levels, and control surfaces.
- Confirm the runway is clear and that the weather is suitable for takeoff.

- **Throttle and Speed**:
    - Gradually advance the throttle to full power, depending on the aircraft. Small planes like the Cessna 172 require around 50-60% throttle to begin rolling.
    - Watch the **airspeed indicator** closely. For most light aircraft, takeoff speed is usually around 60-70 knots, but this can vary based on aircraft type.

- **Lift-Off**:
    - As you reach the recommended takeoff speed, gently pull back on the control yoke to lift the aircraft off the runway.
    - Ensure a smooth, gradual climb rate to maintain control.

- **Climbing**:

- After takeoff, maintain a steady climb by adjusting the throttle and keeping an eye on your altitude and airspeed.
- For larger aircraft, engage the autopilot for altitude and heading hold once you reach your cruising altitude.

2. Flying and Maintaining Altitude

- **Maintain Speed and Altitude:**
    - Use the throttle to adjust speed as needed and adjust the elevator (pitch) to control your climb or descent. For steady flight, keep your aircraft level, with the nose slightly above the horizon.
- **Banking and Turning:**
    - To make turns, bank the aircraft by moving the control yoke or joystick left or right. Keep your turns smooth by maintaining a constant speed and keeping an eye on your bank angle. You may need to apply rudder to coordinate the turn.
- **Leveling Off:**
    - To level off after a climb, reduce throttle slightly and pitch the nose down to maintain a steady altitude. Use the **altimeter** to ensure you're maintaining your target altitude.

3. Landing Like a Pro

Landing is one of the most challenging aspects of flying. Here's how to approach a smooth landing:

- **Approach**:
    - **Speed**: Ensure your speed is within the recommended landing range. Typically, this is around 65-75% of your maximum speed, depending on the aircraft.
    - **Flaps**: Extend the flaps to around 30-40% to help slow the aircraft and create more lift during landing.
    - **Alignment**: Line up with the runway and maintain a stable approach path, keeping your nose slightly above the horizon.
- **Final Approach**:
    - **Glide Path**: Maintain a steady descent rate of around 500 feet per minute. Use the **vertical speed indicator** to keep an eye on your descent rate.
    - **Power Reduction**: As you get closer to the runway, reduce throttle to idle, allowing the aircraft to glide in for a smooth touchdown.
- **Flare and Touchdown**:
    - As you approach the runway, gently pull back on the yoke to initiate the **flare** (raise

the nose slightly). This will soften the landing.

- Touchdown smoothly on the main wheels, keeping the aircraft aligned with the runway centerline.

4. Post-Landing

- **Taxiing**: Once you've landed, reduce speed and retract the flaps. Use the rudder and throttle to taxi the aircraft off the runway and to the designated parking area.

- **Shutdown Procedures**: Follow the aircraft's checklist to safely shut down the engines, close flight instruments, and turn off electrical systems.

Handling Weather and Environmental Factors

Weather plays a huge role in aviation, and *Microsoft Flight Simulator 2024* incorporates real-world weather data to provide a realistic flying experience. Understanding how to handle various weather conditions is essential for every pilot.

1. Wind and Crosswinds

- **Wind Effects**: Wind can significantly affect your flight, especially during takeoff and landing. Crosswinds (winds blowing perpendicular to the runway) are the most challenging, as they can cause the aircraft to drift or veer off course.

- o **Crosswind Landings**: When approaching a runway with a crosswind, use a technique called the **crab method**, where you angle the aircraft slightly into the wind to maintain your course. As you get closer to the runway, apply **side-slip** (using the rudder to align the aircraft with the runway) to touch down smoothly.
- **Wind Shear**: Wind shear occurs when wind speed or direction changes suddenly, particularly at different altitudes. It can cause sudden altitude fluctuations and affect your approach. Always be prepared for unexpected gusts, and keep an eye on airspeed and altitude during the final approach.

2. Turbulence and Storms

- **Turbulence**: In *MSFS 2024*, turbulence is generated by weather systems, air currents, and terrain. Flying through turbulent air can cause your aircraft to bounce or shake, which is more pronounced at higher altitudes.
  - o **Avoiding Turbulence**: Check the weather radar for areas of turbulence. When flying through turbulent areas, reduce your speed to maintain better control, and avoid sharp turns.
- **Thunderstorms**: Thunderstorms can cause severe turbulence, lightning strikes, and intense

rain. Always avoid flying through thunderstorms when possible. If you find yourself caught in one, descend below the storm's base to find smoother air.

3. Low Visibility and Fog

- **Flying in Low Visibility**: In low-visibility conditions, rely on **instrument flight** rather than visual references. Trust your **attitude indicator**, **altimeter**, and **heading indicator** to maintain control and stay on course.

- **Icing Conditions**: Flying in cold weather may lead to ice formation on the wings and tail. This can dramatically affect the aircraft's performance and handling. If you encounter icing, deploy **de-icing systems** (if available) and adjust your altitude to avoid freezing layers of air.

Chapter 5

Advanced Flight Techniques

As you gain experience in *Microsoft Flight Simulator 2024*, it's important to build on your foundational skills by mastering more advanced flight techniques. This section focuses on two primary navigation methods—**Instrument Flight Rules (IFR)** and **Visual Flight Rules (VFR)**—as well as how to manage the aircraft's autopilot and complex flight systems. These skills are essential for flying in real-world conditions and for handling more complex aircraft.

Navigating Using IFR (Instrument Flight Rules)

Instrument Flight Rules (IFR) allow pilots to fly using instruments and navigation systems, without relying on external visual references. IFR is typically used in poor weather conditions or when flying through controlled airspace, such as flying in clouds, fog, or at night. This method is essential for pilots who want to fly through clouds, storms, or low visibility while maintaining safe navigation.

1. Understanding IFR Basics

When flying under IFR, your primary means of navigation are the aircraft's instruments and air traffic control (ATC). The goal is to fly safely while being guided by precise, instrument-based directions.

- **Navigation Aids (NAVAIDs)**: To navigate under IFR, you will primarily rely on the aircraft's onboard **navigation systems** such as:
    - **VOR (VHF Omnidirectional Range)**: Ground-based radio beacons that send out signals, allowing you to tune into the signal and navigate based on your heading relative to the VOR station.
    - **ILS (Instrument Landing System)**: A precision approach system that helps guide you down to the runway during low visibility conditions, providing both lateral and vertical guidance.
    - **GPS and RNAV**: Modern aircraft use **Global Positioning System (GPS)** and **Area Navigation (RNAV)** systems to follow predetermined flight routes more precisely.
- **Altitude and Speed**: Unlike VFR, IFR flight is typically done at **cruising altitudes** where altitude is strictly controlled. ATC will give you altitude assignments, and you must adhere to these instructions to stay in your assigned airspace.

2. Preparing for an IFR Flight

Before you can fly under IFR, you need to plan your route, file an IFR flight plan, and get clearance from ATC. Here's how to prepare for an IFR flight:

- **Flight Planning**: Use the **flight planner** in *MSFS 2024* to set up your IFR route. You'll need to define your departure and destination airports, choose your route based on waypoints, VORs, and airways, and select the appropriate altitudes for your flight.

- **ATC Communication**: Upon receiving your IFR clearance, ATC will provide you with a clearance code, a **route**, and an initial **altitude**. ATC will continuously provide you with headings and altitudes to keep you on course.

- **Check Instruments**: Before departure, make sure the aircraft's **flight instruments** are calibrated and functional. Pay particular attention to the **altimeter**, **heading indicator**, and **attitude indicator**, which are crucial for IFR flight.

3. Flying Under IFR in *MSFS 2024*

- **Following Airway Routes**: After takeoff, engage the autopilot and follow the **waypoints** and **airways** provided by ATC. You will be instructed to fly specific headings and altitudes as you progress along the route.

- o **Navigating via VOR**: Tune into the VOR frequencies for each waypoint. Follow the aircraft's **Navigation Display (ND)** and **Horizon Indicator** to stay aligned with the assigned route.
- o **Altitude Adjustments**: Always follow ATC's instructions for altitude changes. Use the **Vertical Speed Indicator (VSI)** to monitor and adjust your climb or descent rate as needed.
- **Approach and Landing**: As you approach the destination, ATC will guide you to your **Instrument Approach Procedure (IAP)**. This might involve transitioning from a **Standard Terminal Arrival Route (STAR)** to an ILS approach, ensuring a safe landing, especially in low visibility conditions.

Flying in VFR (Visual Flight Rules)

VFR allows pilots to fly using visual references to the ground and other external markers, such as landmarks and the horizon. VFR is the opposite of IFR, as it relies on a pilot's ability to see the environment around them. This method is primarily used in clear weather conditions, and it gives pilots more freedom in choosing their flight path and altitude.

1. Understanding VFR Basics

When flying under VFR, you are responsible for visually avoiding obstacles, other aircraft, and bad weather. This means you need to be aware of your surroundings, including the weather conditions, terrain, and air traffic. Unlike IFR, where instruments are key, VFR relies on **visual cues**.

- **Visual Navigation**: VFR pilots use **landmarks** such as cities, rivers, and mountains to navigate. You can fly from one visible point to another, but you must be able to see the terrain and your surroundings at all times.

- **Weather Conditions**: VFR flight requires good weather with a **ceiling** (cloud cover) and **visibility** that allow you to see the ground. If visibility or cloud cover drops below the VFR minimums, you must switch to IFR.

2. Preparing for a VFR Flight

Before departing under VFR, you should:

- **Flight Planning**: Plan your route based on visible landmarks and available airspace. Set waypoints based on landmarks and ensure that your route avoids restricted or controlled airspace.

- **Weather Considerations**: Check the weather report to ensure it meets VFR criteria. If the weather is too poor, you may need to switch to IFR or delay your flight.

- **ATC Communication**: In controlled airspace, VFR pilots must communicate with ATC for traffic separation and flight instructions. If flying in uncontrolled airspace, you won't be required to communicate with ATC, but it's still a good idea for safety.

3. Flying Under VFR in *MSFS 2024*

- **Navigating Visually**: During VFR flight, you'll rely on landmarks such as highways, rivers, and airports to guide your path. Use the **map** and **radar** to stay on course, and keep your situational awareness high by looking out the windows.

- **Altitude Management**: While VFR flight offers more flexibility, you still need to maintain a safe altitude and be aware of other aircraft. You're required to fly at **minimum safe altitudes** over populated areas or obstacles.

- **Approach and Landing**: When approaching your destination, you'll visually locate the airport, assess the wind conditions, and land accordingly. For small airports, VFR flight may involve using the **traffic pattern** to line up with the runway for landing.

Managing Autopilot and Complex Flight Systems

As you progress to flying more complex aircraft, you'll need to manage autopilot and advanced flight systems.

Autopilot can help reduce workload on long flights, while advanced flight systems help with navigation, engine management, and system monitoring.

1. Autopilot Basics

Autopilot allows you to automate certain aspects of flight, such as altitude control, heading, speed, and navigation. Autopilot is especially useful on long-haul flights or when flying under IFR.

- **Autopilot Modes**:
    - **Altitude Hold**: Maintains the aircraft's current altitude without manual input.
    - **Heading Hold**: Keeps the aircraft flying in the current direction.
    - **Altitude and Heading Control**: Combines altitude and heading hold, allowing for smooth transitions and route tracking.
    - **LNAV/VNAV**: These modes follow **lateral navigation (LNAV)** and **vertical navigation (VNAV)**, useful for following flight plans and managing altitudes and waypoints.
- **Autopilot Setup in *MSFS 2024***:
    - Use the **flight management system (FMS)** to set your waypoints and desired altitudes. You can enter these into the

> autopilot panel, and it will manage your flight automatically.
>
> o For approach, switch to **ILS mode** to allow the autopilot to guide you in for a precision landing.

2. Complex Flight Systems

In more advanced aircraft, you'll need to manage and understand various systems:

- **Flight Management Systems (FMS)**: The FMS is a complex computer system that automates many aspects of flight, including route planning, speed management, and fuel consumption. It's especially useful on commercial jets like the Airbus A320 and Boeing 787.

- **Engines and Fuel Systems**: Understanding engine performance, fuel usage, and managing fuel tanks is essential for long flights. Some aircraft have complex fuel management systems that balance fuel between multiple tanks.

- **Weather Radar and TCAS**: Modern aircraft come with **weather radar** for avoiding storms and **Traffic Collision Avoidance System (TCAS)** to detect nearby aircraft. Learning to use these

Chapter 6

Emergency Procedures: Handling In-Game Crises

In *Microsoft Flight Simulator 2024*, emergencies can arise at any time, and how you respond can make the difference between a safe landing and a disastrous crash. Whether it's an engine failure, turbulence, or storms, understanding how to handle these crises is critical for every pilot. In this section, we will walk you through the essential steps to take in case of these common in-game emergencies.

What to Do in Case of Engine Failures

An engine failure is one of the most serious emergencies you can encounter while flying. *MSFS 2024* simulates realistic engine failures, so it's important to know how to handle the situation when it occurs.

1. Recognizing an Engine Failure

The first sign of an engine failure may be a sudden drop in speed or a reduction in engine RPM. You'll notice this in the **engine gauges**, which may show low oil pressure, high temperature, or no power output at all.

- **Symptoms of Engine Failure**:

- **Sudden loss of power** or a decrease in airspeed
- **Engine instruments in the red** (e.g., low RPM, high temperatures, low oil pressure)
- **Unusual sounds** (e.g., engine sputtering or complete silence)

2. Immediate Actions

Once an engine failure occurs, follow these steps:

- **Maintain Control**:
  - Keep your aircraft level, and don't panic. Use the **attitude indicator** and **airspeed indicator** to maintain a stable flight attitude and speed.
- **Check for Causes**:
  - If you're flying a smaller aircraft, check your **fuel mixture** and ensure the engine isn't running lean. If you're using a multi-engine aircraft, check that the other engine is functioning properly and adjust the throttle settings.
- **Declare an Emergency**:
  - Communicate with **ATC** (Air Traffic Control) and declare an emergency. Use the emergency frequency if necessary, or simply inform ATC of the engine failure.

3. Restarting the Engine (if applicable)

- **Fuel Mixture**: If you're in a small aircraft, adjust the fuel mixture and throttle to attempt an engine restart. Ensure the **fuel selector** is in the correct position (usually "both" or "on" for single-engine aircraft).
- **Engine Restart Procedure**:
    - Switch off the **fuel pump** (if the engine failed due to fuel over-pressurization), set the throttle to idle, and **attempt to restart** the engine using the starter switch.
- **If Restart Fails**:
    - If you cannot restart the engine, begin the emergency landing procedure.

4. Emergency Landing Procedure

- **Glide to Safety**:
    - In case the engine cannot be restarted, choose a suitable **gliding path** to land safely. Small aircraft typically glide at around **65-70 knots** in a neutral descent.
- **Find a Suitable Landing Area**:
    - Look for flat areas, such as fields, roads, or clearings, and avoid power lines or any other obstacles. *MSFS 2024* provides accurate terrain, so identify potential landing spots early.

- **Set Up Your Approach**:
    - When you're within gliding distance of a suitable landing spot, reduce your speed and align with the wind direction for a controlled landing.
- **Flaps**:
    - Use **flaps** if you need to slow down during your approach.
- **Landing**:
    - Perform a **controlled landing** as you would in normal conditions. Once on the ground, taxi to a safe area.

What to Do in Case of Turbulence

Turbulence is a common atmospheric phenomenon that can affect your flight's stability. While turbulence is usually not dangerous, it can be uncomfortable and difficult to manage, especially in smaller aircraft.

1. Recognizing Turbulence

Turbulence occurs when the airflow around the aircraft is disrupted, often due to changes in wind patterns, storms, or passing over mountains. In *MSFS 2024*, turbulence is dynamically generated based on real-world data and weather patterns.

- **Symptoms of Turbulence**:

- **Shaking or bouncing** of the aircraft
- **Changes in altitude** without input from the pilot
- **Speed fluctuations** as the aircraft moves through turbulent air

2. Immediate Actions

- **Maintain Control**:
    - Keep a firm grip on the controls, and avoid overcorrection. Use small, smooth inputs to maintain stability and prevent the aircraft from entering a **spiral dive** or excessive bank.

- **Reduce Speed**:
    - If turbulence is moderate or severe, **reduce speed** to the aircraft's **turbulence penetration speed** (this is typically lower than normal cruising speed). In small aircraft, this is usually around 90-100 knots.

- **Adjust Altitude**:
    - If turbulence is severe at your current altitude, request a change in altitude from ATC. You may be able to climb or descend to a smoother level.

3. Passing Through Severe Turbulence

- **Maintain Level Flight**:
    - During severe turbulence, try to maintain level flight and avoid sudden maneuvers that could destabilize the aircraft. In extreme conditions, the **autopilot** can help keep the aircraft steady, but manual control may be required for better precision.
- **Keep Seatbelts Fastened**:
    - In the real world, ensure your seatbelt is fastened, as turbulence can throw the aircraft out of control momentarily. In *MSFS 2024*, the shaking might cause temporary loss of control, but with proper technique, you should be able to maintain stability.

What to Do in Case of Storms

Flying through storms can be challenging and dangerous. In *MSFS 2024*, storms are simulated realistically, complete with **lightning**, **rain**, **hail**, and **wind shear**. Proper storm management techniques are essential for safe navigation.

1. Recognizing Storms

Storms are characterized by thick, dark clouds (cumulonimbus), intense winds, and turbulence. *MSFS 2024* uses live weather data to simulate these conditions, so you may encounter severe weather, especially at certain altitudes or during specific in-game missions.

- **Symptoms of Storms**:
    - **Heavy rain** and **reduced visibility**
    - **Intense turbulence** and **wind gusts**
    - **Lightning strikes** in the distance
    - **Low cloud cover** and **cloud formations** signaling an active storm

2. **Immediate Actions**

- **Weather Radar**:
    - Use the **weather radar** (if equipped) to scan for areas of heavy precipitation, turbulence, and storms. This allows you to make informed decisions about whether to reroute or avoid the storm.
- **Divert or Avoid the Storm**:
    - If the storm is unavoidable, try to **maneuver around** it by changing course. Use the **autopilot** and navigation systems to help you stay on course as you fly through turbulent areas.
    - In severe cases, consider requesting a **diversion** to another airport or a safer flight level from ATC.
- **Prepare for Thunderstorms**:

- If you're already in the storm, reduce your speed to the **turbulence penetration speed** and use **autopilot** or manual control to stabilize the aircraft.

3. Handling Lightning and Hail

- **Lightning**:
    - Lightning rarely causes damage to aircraft but can make navigation difficult due to temporary **visibility loss**. Focus on your instruments and remain calm.

- **Hail**:
    - If hail is detected, it's crucial to **descend below** the storm's base to avoid significant damage. Avoid flying through areas where hail is reported, and change altitude or route to stay clear of it.

4. Approach and Landing in Stormy Conditions

- **ILS Approach**:
    - In storms with heavy rain and low visibility, switch to **Instrument Landing System (ILS)** for an automated approach to ensure you stay aligned with the runway.

- **Wind Gusts**:
    - Be prepared for gusty crosswinds during approach. Use the **crab method** for

crosswind landings, and keep your **nose aligned** with the runway as you approach.

- **Reduced Visibility**:
    - Fly the aircraft using **instrument references** and trust your autopilot for landing assistance if visibility is extremely poor.

Chapter 7

Exploration & Missions

One of the most captivating aspects of *Microsoft Flight Simulator 2024* is its vast and beautifully rendered world. Whether you want to simply explore breathtaking scenery, visit famous landmarks, or engage in immersive missions, the game offers an unparalleled flying experience. With detailed global mapping, realistic atmospheric phenomena, and dynamic weather, the game brings every corner of the Earth to life. In this section, we'll explore how to maximize your exploration experience, discover iconic landmarks, and enjoy the richness of the world in the game.

Explore the World: The Ultimate Flight Experience

Flying in *Microsoft Flight Simulator 2024* isn't just about controlling an aircraft—it's about the adventure of exploring the planet from above. The game's extensive world map, fueled by live weather data and high-resolution satellite imagery, ensures that every flight feels unique and that the world constantly evolves.

1. Global Mapping: An Expansive World Awaits

The global mapping in *MSFS 2024* is nothing short of revolutionary, offering photorealistic imagery and topographic accuracy that enables a truly immersive flying experience. The world is accurately modeled, and players can fly anywhere—from major metropolitan cities to remote islands, vast deserts, and towering mountain ranges.

- **Satellite Imagery**: The game utilizes cutting-edge satellite imagery and photogrammetry to replicate real-world terrain in stunning detail. As you fly, you'll notice that the landscape below you looks just like it does in real life, from city streets to forests, rivers, and coastlines.

- **Dynamic Terrain**: The terrain evolves as you fly, with mountains, valleys, plains, and water bodies reflecting the unique geography of each region. The game updates the world regularly, ensuring that any changes in the real world, such as new buildings or natural events, are accurately represented.

- **Interactive World**: You can seamlessly zoom into cities or explore natural wonders. The game's integration with real-world data allows you to see not just static landscapes but **seasonal changes**, **wildlife patterns**, and even **real-time traffic**.

2. Flight Planning and Exploration

- **World Map Interface**: Use the interactive world map to plan your flights. You can fly freely without a flight plan, but setting a route to your desired destination—whether it's a nearby landmark or a distant city—can add purpose to your exploration.

- **Custom Routes and Waypoints**: For more advanced exploration, create custom flight plans with specific waypoints that lead you over picturesque areas, famous landmarks, or even remote locations. Customize your flight plan by selecting **VOR stations**, **airways**, and **waypoints**, allowing you to explore in a more structured way.

- **Explore by Flight Type**: You can explore the world in different ways—taking off from a small private airport, flying commercial jets across continents, or even piloting helicopters and smaller aircraft to get closer to the ground and explore in detail.

Discovering Iconic Landmarks and Cities

Microsoft Flight Simulator 2024 offers the ability to visit some of the world's most iconic landmarks and cities. Thanks to real-world data, you can fly over **famous landmarks** and **breathtaking cities**, seeing them from the unique perspective of the cockpit.

1. Famous Landmarks to Visit

Here are just a few of the iconic landmarks you can visit, thanks to the detailed global mapping system in *MSFS 2024*:

- **The Eiffel Tower** (Paris, France): Take a flight over the city of Paris, and enjoy a breathtaking view of the **Eiffel Tower**. Fly beneath its structure or soar high above the iconic landmark for a bird's-eye view of the French capital.

- **Grand Canyon** (Arizona, USA): The **Grand Canyon** is one of the most stunning natural formations in the world. Fly along the canyon's edge, descend into the valley, or perform an aerial loop to admire the intricate rock formations.

- **Machu Picchu** (Peru): Fly over the famous **Machu Picchu** ruins nestled high in the Andes. The lush green mountains surrounding this ancient site provide a spectacular backdrop for aerial exploration.

- **The Pyramids of Giza** (Cairo, Egypt): Soar over the historic **Pyramids of Giza** and the Sphinx, taking in the grand scale of these monumental structures. The vast Egyptian desert provides an awe-inspiring contrast to the ancient wonders.

- **Mount Everest** (Nepal): If you're an experienced pilot, navigate your way to the **Himalayas** and attempt to climb to the highest point on Earth— **Mount Everest**. The surrounding peaks and valleys are just as awe-inspiring from the air as they are on the ground.

- **The Great Wall of China** (China): The **Great Wall of China** stretches over 13,000 miles, and from above, you can follow its course as it winds its way through the mountains. This incredible structure is one of the most recognizable landmarks in the world.

2. Iconic Cities to Explore

Take to the skies and explore the most iconic cities around the globe, including:

- **New York City, USA**: The skyline of New York City is one of the most recognizable in the world. Fly past the **Statue of Liberty**, **Empire State Building**, and **Central Park**, or approach **LaGuardia Airport** for a dramatic city approach.

- **Tokyo, Japan**: Soar over the buzzing streets of Tokyo and see iconic landmarks such as **Tokyo Tower**, the **Shibuya Crossing**, and the **Skytree**. The contrast of modern skyscrapers and traditional temples makes Tokyo a fascinating city to explore.

- **London, UK**: Fly over **Big Ben**, the **London Eye**, and **Tower Bridge**. The historic Thames River snakes through the city, offering plenty of navigation points and visual landmarks to admire from above.

- **Dubai, UAE**: Marvel at the futuristic skyline of Dubai, with landmarks like the **Burj Khalifa** and **Palm Jumeirah**. Dubai's rapid urbanization offers a unique aerial view as you navigate this city of innovation.

- **Sydney, Australia**: Discover the stunning beauty of **Sydney**, including its famous **Opera House** and **Harbour Bridge**. The city's stunning coastline and beaches offer amazing vistas from the air.
- **Rio de Janeiro, Brazil**: Fly over **Christ the Redeemer** on **Corcovado Mountain** and explore the stunning beaches of **Copacabana** and **Ipanema**. The rugged hills surrounding Rio make for a thrilling and scenic flying experience.

Detailed Global Mapping and Atmospheric Phenomena

In *Microsoft Flight Simulator 2024*, every flight is impacted by the game's **realistic global mapping** and dynamic **atmospheric phenomena**, providing a highly immersive and ever-changing flying experience.

1. Dynamic Weather and Real-Time Atmospheric Conditions

The weather system in *MSFS 2024* is powered by live data, which means that real-world weather patterns affect your flight. You can fly in anything from **clear skies** to **violent storms**, with real-time updates to wind, temperature, and cloud cover.

- **Cloud Formation and Types**: Weather is dynamic, so clouds form and dissipate in real-time. From **cumulus clouds** on a calm day to **cumulonimbus storms**, each cloud type impacts how you fly and how you need to manage your aircraft.

- **Turbulence and Wind**: Wind speeds and directions are constantly changing, and flying in turbulence can provide a thrilling challenge. In areas like **mountain ranges** or **coastal regions**, you may encounter unpredictable turbulence, making it crucial to adjust your altitude and speed.

- **Storms and Lightning**: *MSFS 2024* accurately simulates **thunderstorms**, **rain**, **snow**, and **lightning**. These atmospheric conditions can drastically affect visibility, aircraft handling, and flight planning. It's important to plan for **weather delays**, use **radar** to avoid severe weather, and **adjust flight plans** accordingly.

2. Seasonal Changes and Time of Day

The game features **seasonal changes**, which means that the world transforms with each season. Fly over **snow-covered** mountains in winter, or witness vibrant **autumn foliage** as trees change color. The **time of day** also plays a crucial role in how the world looks and feels.

- **Day-Night Cycle**: As the day progresses, the lighting in the game shifts, casting long shadows during sunrise and sunset, and creating stunning visual effects as you fly at night.

- **Seasons and Weather Variability**: During winter months, snow will blanket the ground, and you'll see winter weather patterns like snowflakes and ice on the plane's windshield. In the summer, explore lush green landscapes and sunny skies.

3. Realistic Ocean and River Systems

The game's depiction of **oceans** and **rivers** is just as detailed as its landmasses. You'll notice the true-to-life behavior of the water, from **ocean waves** to **tidal movements** in coastal regions. Rivers wind through landscapes, offering perfect routes for exploration or scenic flights.

Chapter 8

Missions & Challenges: Taking Your Skills Further

Microsoft Flight Simulator 2024 offers a wide range of missions and challenges that allow you to push your piloting skills to the next level. These missions provide an exciting way to practice what you've learned, explore new regions, and tackle real-world aviation scenarios. Whether you're flying a rescue operation, taking in the views on a scenic flight, or attempting more complex tasks, these missions will test your ability to handle various flight conditions and objectives.

In this section, we'll explore the different types of missions you can engage in, how to complete them, and the rewards that come with mastering these challenges.

Engaging in Rescue Operations, Scenic Flights, and More

1. Rescue Operations

One of the most thrilling aspects of *MSFS 2024* is its collection of **rescue operations** that simulate real-world emergency response scenarios. These missions test your skills in navigating difficult terrain, managing unpredictable weather, and making critical decisions under pressure.

- **Search and Rescue (SAR)**: In these missions, you are tasked with locating stranded individuals, often in remote or hazardous locations. These missions can involve flying over mountainous terrain, across oceans, or even navigating through fog and storms. You'll need to use **visual clues**, **radar**, and **infrared sensors** (if available) to locate the target.

- **Helicopter Rescue**: Some rescue missions require you to fly helicopters, where you must pick up passengers or cargo from difficult-to-reach locations. Whether it's rescuing stranded mountain climbers or delivering supplies to remote islands, helicopter rescue missions require precise flying skills, especially in turbulent conditions.

- **Air Ambulance**: These missions involve transporting injured passengers to the nearest hospital, often under tight time constraints. You'll need to manage speed, altitude, and approach precision while navigating through busy airspace and possibly avoiding bad weather conditions.

- **Disaster Relief**: Delivering emergency supplies or personnel to disaster-stricken areas is another form of rescue operation. These missions often involve flying into areas with limited infrastructure or challenging weather conditions.

The focus here is on **timely delivery**, **resource management**, and **handling of large payloads**.

2. Scenic Flights

For those who want to enjoy the beauty of the world from the skies, **scenic flights** are an excellent way to experience the majesty of the planet's most iconic landmarks, natural wonders, and serene landscapes.

- **Famous Landmarks and City Tours**: These flights take you over famous cities like **New York, Paris,** and **Tokyo,** where you can enjoy panoramic views of the skyline, monuments, and surrounding landscapes. Scenic flights can also focus on natural wonders such as the **Grand Canyon, Amazon Rainforest**, or the **Alps**.

- **Flight Tours**: These missions are designed for players who want to explore specific regions or countries. You'll fly over picturesque areas, experiencing different environments and weather conditions. These flights can range from short local tours to extensive cross-country flights.

- **Island Hopping**: In areas like the **Caribbean** or **Pacific Islands**, scenic flights may involve island-hopping across a group of tropical islands, where you'll see clear water, beaches, and remote locations. This is perfect for light aircraft or helicopters and offers breathtaking views.

- **Mountain Flights**: Fly through the most challenging and scenic mountain ranges, such as the **Himalayas, Rockies**, or **Andes**. These missions will test your ability to navigate narrow valleys and steep cliffs while enjoying some of the most stunning landscapes the world has to offer.

3. Delivery and Transport Missions

In these missions, you're tasked with transporting goods or people to different locations under specific conditions. It's a great way to practice flight planning, cargo management, and route optimization.

- **Cargo Delivery**: Whether it's shipping critical goods to a remote location or transporting hazardous materials, cargo delivery missions challenge you to load and balance your aircraft, plan efficient routes, and ensure safe delivery.
- **Passenger Transport**: Fly groups of passengers between cities or to secluded airstrips. These missions often require you to handle customer service expectations, flight time management, and smooth approaches into busy or small airports.

Earning Rewards and Completing Objectives

Completing missions in *Microsoft Flight Simulator 2024* not only provides a sense of accomplishment but also rewards you with in-game **currency**, **achievements**, and **customization options** that enhance your flying experience.

1. Earning Rewards

- **Mission-Based Rewards**: After completing a mission, you'll receive rewards based on your performance. These rewards can include:
    - **Experience Points (XP)**: Gain XP for completing various flight tasks. The more efficient and precise your flight, the more XP you will earn. XP can be used to unlock new aircraft, flight challenges, or customization options.
    - **Currency**: Some missions award you **in-game currency**, which can be spent on new planes, liveries, or flight upgrades.
    - **Aircraft Unlocks**: Completing specific missions or challenges will unlock new aircraft, allowing you to expand your fleet. This might include special helicopters, experimental aircraft, or premium planes.
- **Achievements**: As you complete different missions and challenges, you'll unlock achievements. These may include milestones like completing a certain number of rescue missions, flying a set number of hours, or exploring specific geographic regions. Each achievement is a badge of honor and a testament to your progress as a pilot.

2. Completing Objectives

Most missions and challenges in *MSFS 2024* come with specific objectives that you must complete to achieve success. These objectives help guide your flight, providing direction and purpose. Objectives include:

- **Timed Objectives**: Some missions require you to complete a task within a specific time limit, such as delivering cargo or performing a rescue within a set window.

- **Navigation Objectives**: Many missions involve flying between multiple waypoints, where you need to maintain accurate heading, altitude, and speed. Completing these objectives ensures you're following your flight plan and staying on course.

- **Handling Environmental Factors**: Some missions require you to navigate in challenging weather conditions, such as storms, turbulence, or night flights. These scenarios test your ability to adapt and manage the aircraft under less-than-ideal circumstances.

- **Skill-Based Objectives**: Challenges like **precision landings**, **low-altitude flying**, or **formation flying** require you to demonstrate specific piloting skills. Successfully completing these tasks will reward you with recognition and XP.

3. Customizing and Upgrading Your Aircraft

With the rewards you earn, you can customize and upgrade your aircraft for better performance, appearance, or functionality. This includes:

- **Livery Customization**: Unlock and apply custom liveries for your aircraft, giving it a unique look for every flight. You can personalize your planes with custom designs or choose from various pre-made themes available in the marketplace.

- **Aircraft Upgrades**: Enhance your aircraft's performance by upgrading specific systems such as engines, avionics, and autopilot. Some missions may unlock upgrades or provide the option to adjust settings for optimal flight performance.

- **Flight Gear**: As you progress, you can also unlock additional flight gear such as new instruments for your cockpit, flight plan options, and unique accessories.

Multiplayer & Community Features

Microsoft Flight Simulator 2024 takes your flying experience beyond solo missions by offering robust **multiplayer** and **community** features that connect you with pilots worldwide. Whether you're teaming up with friends for a casual flight, competing in live events, or tackling global challenges, these features add layers of excitement, camaraderie, and competition to your aviation journey. Let's explore how you can fly with others and take part in the broader *MSFS 2024* community.

Flying with Friends: Multiplayer Mode

One of the most engaging aspects of *Microsoft Flight Simulator 2024* is the ability to fly together in **multiplayer mode**. This feature allows you to share the skies with fellow pilots, participate in group flights, and experience the thrill of flying in a real-world environment alongside friends or strangers.

1. Joining Multiplayer Sessions

- **Global Multiplayer Network**: *MSFS 2024* offers a dynamic global multiplayer network where you can join open or private sessions. Whether you're exploring the world together or participating in group events, multiplayer mode allows you to share the skies with others in real-time.

- **Flight Plans in Multiplayer**: As part of the multiplayer session, you can set up a shared flight plan, allowing your friends to follow the same route, whether it's a short hop across a country or a long-haul transcontinental flight.

- **Cooperative Flying**: In multiplayer mode, you can fly as a team. Whether you're piloting a **helicopter rescue** mission together or performing a formation flight, cooperative multiplayer lets you collaborate on missions and flights. You can help guide each other to waypoints, share information, or navigate through challenging weather conditions as a group.

2. Customizing Multiplayer Settings

- **Private Flights**: If you prefer to fly only with your friends, you can set up a **private multiplayer session**. This ensures you have full control over who joins the session and can ensure that only invited players are part of the flight. You can also restrict the session to a specific aircraft type or region to make the experience more enjoyable.

- **Public Flights**: If you're looking to meet new people and share the sky with a larger group, you can join **public flights** where you'll encounter a mix of other players flying at the same time. These sessions can be chaotic but exciting, as you'll witness aircraft of all types flying together.

3. Shared Aircraft and Formation Flying

- **Shared Aircraft**: In multiplayer mode, you can share the same aircraft with a friend in **co-pilot mode**. If you're flying a complex aircraft like an **Airbus A320** or **Boeing 787**, you can take turns controlling the aircraft, helping each other navigate the flight and manage the systems.

- **Formation Flying**: For those looking for precision, multiplayer mode also supports **formation flying**, where you and your friends can fly closely together, maintaining perfect alignment and synchronization. This requires good communication and precision flying skills, but it's an incredibly rewarding experience.

Connecting with Fellow Pilots Online

Microsoft Flight Simulator 2024 provides several ways to connect with fellow pilots, whether you're looking to engage in a casual flight, compete in challenges, or simply meet like-minded individuals who share your passion for aviation.

1. Flight Planning and Sharing

- **Collaborative Flight Planning**: *MSFS 2024* includes integrated tools that allow you to plan flights together with other players. You can share flight plans, set waypoints, and adjust the route in real time. This makes flying in multiplayer sessions more engaging, as you can work together to follow a specific route or fly to a common destination.

- **Real-Time Flight Sharing**: Share your flight progress with others through live tracking. This allows your friends and fellow pilots to follow your journey as you fly, and you can coordinate with them if they need to adjust their route to join up with you.

2. In-Game Communication

- **Voice and Text Chat**: While flying in multiplayer mode, communication is key. *MSFS 2024* supports **voice and text chat**, allowing pilots to communicate in real-time. You can talk to your co-pilot, discuss your next waypoint with friends, or join group discussions about the weather or flight conditions. Voice communication is especially useful in dynamic group flights or formation flying.

- **ATC and Player Communication**: You can communicate with **ATC** during multiplayer flights, and your fellow pilots will hear your ATC communications if they are in range. This can add an additional layer of realism to your flights, especially in busy airports or when flying in controlled airspace.

3. Community and Events

- **Community Hub**: Join the official *MSFS 2024* community hub to connect with pilots, share flight experiences, and participate in discussions. The community hub is the place to find useful guides, tutorials, and flight recommendations from other players.

- **Flying Clubs**: In *MSFS 2024*, you can join virtual flying clubs where members regularly meet to engage in multiplayer sessions, take part in community challenges, or simply fly together for fun. These clubs offer a sense of camaraderie and provide opportunities to meet new people and improve your flying skills.

Participating in Live Events and Global Challenges

To add excitement and a sense of achievement, *MSFS 2024* offers **live events** and **global challenges** that you can participate in. These events and challenges are designed to test your piloting skills, whether you're flying solo or in multiplayer groups, and they offer rewards based on your performance.

1. Live Events

Live events in *MSFS 2024* are real-time occurrences that allow you to participate in global challenges or time-limited missions. These events can range from **scenic tours** to **disaster relief flights**, and they often feature different locations, aircraft, and weather conditions.

- **Featured Events**: *MSFS 2024* regularly features **special events**, such as **historic flights**, **sponsored air races**, or **expeditions** to remote regions. These events offer a unique opportunity to participate in an exciting, time-limited mission with players around the world.

- **Interactive Leaderboards**: During live events, you can track your performance through **leaderboards**, which show how you rank against other players. Whether it's a time challenge or precision landing competition, these live events create a sense of community and friendly competition.

- **Seasonal Challenges**: Participate in events based around **holidays**, **weather conditions**, or **special aviation milestones**. These challenges often have specific aircraft or route requirements and provide unique rewards for completion.

2. Global Challenges

Global challenges are more long-term events that test your skills over extended periods. These challenges are designed for players who want to engage in multi-leg flights or complete a series of missions.

- **The World Tour**: One of the most iconic global challenges is the **World Tour**, where players attempt to fly around the world, completing legs of a journey that take them through different continents and climates. Players can follow preset routes or customize their journey based on their preferences.

- **Time Trials**: Compete in **time trials** where you must complete a set route within a certain timeframe. The challenge lies in your ability to navigate accurately, optimize speed, and manage fuel effectively.

- **Weather-Based Challenges**: Tackle **weather challenges**, where you fly through various weather phenomena, such as heavy storms, crosswinds, or turbulence. These challenges test your ability to fly under challenging conditions.

3. Rewards for Participation

Participating in live events and global challenges often comes with **rewards**, which can include:

- **Achievements and Badges**: Unlock new achievements or badges for completing specific missions, challenges, or event milestones.

- **Exclusive Aircraft and Liveries**: Some events unlock special aircraft or liveries that are only available to participants, allowing you to add unique items to your fleet.

- **Experience Points and Currency**: Earning XP and in-game currency is a common reward, which you can use to unlock new aircraft, customize existing ones, or purchase additional content.

Chapter 9

Live Weather and Real-World Traffic

One of the standout features of *Microsoft Flight Simulator 2024* is its ability to integrate **live weather** and **real-world traffic** into the game, making your flying experience as immersive and dynamic as possible. These live features ensure that the world you fly through reflects the conditions of the real world, creating a more authentic and ever-changing environment. In this section, we'll explore how live weather and real-world traffic work in *MSFS 2024*, and how you can use these features to maximize your immersion.

Enhancing Your Flight with Real-World Data

1. Live Weather: A Dynamic, Real-Time Experience

Live weather in *MSFS 2024* pulls data from real-world weather systems to create a highly dynamic environment. The game constantly updates weather conditions based on real-time data, ensuring that no two flights are ever the same. Whether you're flying through clear skies, dealing with turbulent weather, or navigating through a storm, live weather enhances the realism of your flights.

- **Real-Time Weather Data**: The game sources live weather data from **National Weather Service (NWS)** and other global weather agencies. This means that you're flying with the same weather that's affecting real-world airports and airspace at the time of your flight.
    - **Clouds and Precipitation**: Realistic cloud formations and precipitation patterns make each flight visually stunning and immersive. Expect to see heavy rainstorms, fog, or perfect clear skies, depending on where you're flying.
    - **Wind and Temperature**: Live wind conditions and temperature changes add further realism to your flight. Be prepared to adjust your speed and altitude to accommodate sudden wind shifts or turbulence, and monitor temperature changes that affect aircraft performance, especially at high altitudes.
    - **Thunderstorms and Lightning**: In stormy conditions, you'll encounter realistic **lightning, turbulence**, and **wind shear**. These can make flying challenging but exciting, requiring you to use your piloting skills to manage the aircraft safely.

- **Seasonal Changes**: Just like in the real world, *MSFS 2024* reflects seasonal weather changes. For example, you may experience snow in the winter months or wildfires in areas where they occur in real life, all simulated in real-time.

2. Live Weather Effects on Flight Performance

The live weather system significantly impacts flight performance, requiring pilots to adjust their flying techniques. Some key effects of live weather include:

- **Turbulence**: Flying through **turbulent air** can affect the smoothness of your flight, especially when flying near mountains, in thunderstorms, or in areas of thermal updrafts. Pay attention to weather patterns and adjust your altitude or speed accordingly to manage turbulence.

- **Wind and Crosswinds**: Wind can impact your approach and landing. Strong **crosswinds** during landing require a more advanced flying technique to keep the aircraft aligned with the runway. Be prepared to apply **crab landings** or **side-slips** to counteract the wind.

- **Visibility**: Weather like **fog, rain**, and **snow** can reduce visibility, forcing you to rely more heavily on **instrument flying** (IFR). It can also affect your approach and landing, especially in airports without Instrument Landing Systems (ILS).

- **Temperature and Air Density**: Changes in temperature and air pressure will affect the aircraft's **engine performance** and **lift**. In colder weather, the aircraft's engines may perform more efficiently, while hot weather can reduce engine power and lift, requiring adjustments in your flight plan or speed.

How to Maximize Your Immersion Using Live Features

To get the most out of *Microsoft Flight Simulator 2024's* live features, you need to understand how to incorporate **live weather** and **real-world traffic** into your flights. These features make the experience feel more connected to the real world, adding layers of depth and realism to your flight.

1. Using Live Weather to Enhance Immersion

To make your flights as realistic as possible, consider the following tips for utilizing the live weather system:

- **Pre-Flight Weather Check**: Before starting your flight, check the weather conditions at your departure and destination airports. You can access real-time weather reports through the game's map interface or external tools like weather apps or websites.
    - **Plan for Adverse Conditions**: If you're flying in an area with bad weather, adjust your flight plan to accommodate turbulence or visibility issues. For example, if there's heavy fog, you might

opt for an ILS approach or adjust your flight altitude to avoid fog layers.

- **In-Flight Adjustments**: As you fly, monitor the weather and be prepared for unexpected changes. Winds may pick up, storms could form, or visibility could deteriorate, requiring quick decisions about altitude, route, and speed.
  - **Adjust Flight Path**: Use **ATC communication** or the in-game radar to adjust your flight path and avoid hazardous weather areas, such as thunderstorms or severe turbulence.
  - **Maintain Situational Awareness**: Keep a close eye on weather radar, airspeed, and altitude. Sudden weather changes can create challenges, so being proactive and maintaining awareness of your surroundings is essential.
- **Weather-Based Challenges**: Embrace the weather by taking on specific **weather-based challenges**. For example, try landing in heavy rain, fly through a snowstorm, or take on a crosswind landing challenge. This will not only enhance your skills but also add variety to your flying experience.

2. Live Traffic: Real-World Air Traffic in Your Flight

MSFS 2024 incorporates **real-world traffic**, simulating other aircraft flying in the same airspace. You'll encounter commercial flights, private aircraft, and even general aviation planes, making your experience feel alive and interactive.

- **Real-World Air Traffic**: With live traffic enabled, you'll see **real-world aircraft** following real-time flight schedules and routes. These aircraft will appear in your vicinity and follow similar flight paths, adding realism to your flying experience.
    - o **Monitor Traffic**: Keep track of **air traffic control (ATC)** communications and make adjustments as needed to avoid other aircraft in your path. This creates a more dynamic and realistic flying environment, especially near busy airports or during group flights.
- **Air Traffic and Airport Management**: If you're landing at a major airport, you may encounter a variety of other aircraft in your landing pattern, including large commercial airliners and smaller general aviation planes. Follow the air traffic patterns and communicate with ATC to ensure safe landing procedures.
- **AI Traffic (Offline)**: If you prefer not to engage with live traffic, *MSFS 2024* offers an **AI traffic system** that generates aircraft based on typical flight patterns. This system allows you to experience a lively atmosphere even when you're not connected to the internet or in multiplayer mode.

3. Integrating Live Weather with Multiplayer Flights

When flying with others in **multiplayer mode**, live weather makes every flight unique. Here's how you can enhance your multiplayer experience:

- **Synchronize Flight Plans**: In multiplayer, you and your friends can fly in the same weather conditions, making every flight an authentic shared experience. If one pilot encounters turbulence, everyone else will feel it as well, creating a shared challenge.

- **Cooperative Weather Navigation**: In multiplayer flights, work together with fellow pilots to navigate around storms, monitor weather patterns, and communicate any changes in the flight conditions. This adds an element of teamwork to your flying.

- **Live Weather Events**: Participate in **live weather events** where players can join together to tackle difficult conditions. These events might include challenges like flying through thunderstorms, completing ILS approaches during low visibility, or navigating high winds at takeoff and landing.

Chapter 10

Training & Flight School

Microsoft Flight Simulator 2024 offers an interactive and comprehensive flight school to help both new and experienced pilots develop their skills. The training system provides a step-by-step learning experience, guiding you through the fundamentals of flying, mastering advanced maneuvers, and preparing for more complex aircraft. Whether you're starting with basic maneuvers or want to master an airliner, *MSFS 2024* provides specialized lessons to enhance your piloting skills.

Interactive Training: A Step-by-Step Learning Experience

The training system in *MSFS 2024* is designed to take you from basic concepts to advanced piloting techniques, all in an immersive and guided way. The interactive training program helps you learn by actually flying the aircraft, receiving real-time feedback, and mastering essential skills through hands-on practice.

1. Training Modules and Guided Lessons

MSFS 2024 includes a series of training modules that break down essential flight skills. These lessons are interactive and provide a structured learning environment:

- **Fundamentals of Flight**: The training starts with basic concepts, such as how an aircraft works, how to control it, and how to take off and land safely. These lessons include practical exercises, like flying a **Cessna 172** through basic maneuvers and understanding the **instruments** in the cockpit.

- **Takeoff and Landing**: Once you have the basics down, the training focuses on takeoff and landing procedures. These lessons will guide you through everything from **clearing the runway** to executing smooth landings in varying conditions (wind, rain, visibility).

- **Flight Stability and Control**: In these lessons, you'll practice maintaining **altitude**, **airspeed**, and **heading** in different flight scenarios. You'll learn how to **trim** the aircraft for smooth flight and handle the plane during turbulence and weather shifts.

2. Interactive Features

The beauty of interactive training is that you learn by actually doing the tasks. The lessons are designed to give you practical skills, while also providing in-game tools to enhance the experience:

- **Step-by-Step Guidance**: As you fly, you'll receive step-by-step instructions on what to do next, such as how to climb, descend, or perform a turn. This guidance helps you understand the sequence of actions necessary for each task.

- **Real-Time Feedback**: During training, the game provides real-time feedback on your actions. For example, if you're climbing too steeply or your speed is too low during a turn, the game will alert you and provide suggestions for improvement. This allows you to correct mistakes and learn from them on the spot.

- **Replays and Analysis**: After completing each training mission, you can replay the flight, review your actions, and analyze areas for improvement. This feature is particularly useful for refining techniques or understanding where you went wrong.

Mastering Your First Solo Flight

After completing the initial training lessons, you'll be ready for your **first solo flight**. This is a significant milestone in your piloting journey, as it involves flying the aircraft on your own, using the skills you've acquired in training.

1. Building Confidence

Before your solo flight, you'll have practiced key maneuvers, navigation, and aircraft control under the supervision of an instructor. Your first solo flight involves applying these skills while being free from external guidance.

- **Pre-Flight Checklist**: Before your solo flight, review the **pre-flight checklist** to ensure the aircraft is ready for departure. This includes inspecting fuel levels, engine performance, control surfaces, and instruments.

- **Solo Flight Objectives**: Your first solo flight is often a simple loop or circuit around the airfield, where you practice basic maneuvers like taking off, climbing, turning, and landing. You may also be tasked with performing a **touch-and-go**—a procedure where you land on the runway and immediately take off again to practice multiple landings.

2. Self-Assessment and Feedback

After completing your solo flight, you'll assess your performance and receive feedback from the training system:

- **Self-Evaluation**: Reflect on the flight, noting areas where you felt confident and areas where you struggled. Did you maintain a steady altitude? Were your landings smooth?

- **Instructor Feedback**: While there is no actual instructor during the solo flight, the game provides feedback on your performance. For instance, if your approach was too steep, the system will provide suggestions for smoother landings next time.

- **Flight Logs**: You'll be able to access your flight logs, which document your solo flight experience, along with any corrections or improvements that need to be made.

Specialized Lessons for Different Aircraft and Maneuvers

Once you've mastered basic flight skills, it's time to move on to more specialized lessons. These lessons cover a variety of aircraft types and advanced maneuvers, allowing you to broaden your piloting expertise.

1. Small Aircraft Training

- **General Aviation (GA) Lessons**: In these lessons, you'll learn how to operate light aircraft such as the **Cessna 172** or **Piper Cub**. These aircraft are ideal for learning the fundamentals, but they also offer opportunities to practice more advanced maneuvers like **aerobatics**, **navigation** using **VORs**, and **short field landings**.
- **Maneuvers in GA Aircraft**: Training in small aircraft focuses on basic maneuvers such as:
    - **Stalls**: Practice recovering from **power-off stalls** and **power-on stalls** to simulate real-world emergency scenarios.

- **Slow Flight**: Fly at low speeds while maintaining control of the aircraft, a critical skill for landing and maneuvering in tight spaces.
- **Steep Turns**: Learn to perform steep, controlled turns at high angles of bank, which is useful for navigating tight airspace or landing patterns.

2. Commercial Aircraft Training

- **Multi-Crew Operations**: Flying a commercial jet like the **Airbus A320** or **Boeing 787** requires a completely different skill set. These lessons focus on the operation of **advanced avionics**, **autopilot systems**, and **flight management systems (FMS)**.
- **Complex Maneuvers**: Training for commercial aircraft involves learning:
  - **ILS Approaches**: Using the **Instrument Landing System (ILS)** for precision approaches in low visibility conditions.
  - **Autopilot Usage**: Mastering **autopilot functions**, including altitude hold, heading, and speed management. This allows for smoother, more accurate long-haul flights.
  - **Airways and Route Planning**: Learn how to navigate **airways**, **waypoints**, and

flight plans, making use of **RNAV** and **VOR** navigation.

3. Advanced Maneuvers and Emergency Training

Once you've gained confidence in basic flight and commercial aircraft, specialized lessons can be taken to master complex maneuvers and emergency procedures.

- **Emergency Landing Training**: Practice emergency landing scenarios in both small and commercial aircraft. This includes handling engine failures, severe turbulence, and navigating to emergency landing fields or alternate airports.

- **Formation Flying**: Learn the skills required to fly in tight formation with other aircraft, which requires precise control, coordination, and constant communication between pilots.

- **Night Flying**: Develop your skills for flying at night or in low-visibility conditions. Training includes using **instrument flight rules (IFR)** and managing navigation with minimal external visual references.

4. Specialized Aircraft and Helicopter Training

- **Helicopter Lessons**: If you want to experience vertical flight, *MSFS 2024* offers lessons for helicopters, such as the **Bell 407**. Flying a helicopter involves unique techniques like **hovering**, **tail rotor control**, and **vertical landings**.

- **Private Jet Training**: For players interested in flying jets, the game offers lessons on smaller **private jets**, teaching you how to operate high-performance, high-speed aircraft and navigate through busy airspace.

Chapter 11

Advanced Flight Schools and Add-ons

Microsoft Flight Simulator 2024 not only provides a robust in-game training system but also offers avenues for **advanced flight schools** and **third-party content** that can enhance the learning experience for expert pilots. These external resources and add-ons provide deeper, more specialized training, realistic aircraft models, and unique flying environments, allowing you to further hone your skills and challenge yourself with professional-grade content.

Third-Party Content for Expert Pilots

For experienced pilots seeking additional depth in their training or looking to expand their aircraft fleet, *MSFS 2024* supports **third-party content**. These add-ons can range from **aircraft** and **scenery enhancements** to **flight training modules** and **realistic flight dynamics**.

1. Accessing Third-Party Aircraft

Third-party aircraft models are one of the most popular types of content for expert pilots. These aircraft add more variety and realism to your flights, ranging from vintage planes to modern jets, helicopters, and even experimental aircraft.

- **Custom Aircraft Models**: Many third-party developers create highly detailed and realistic aircraft that are often not available in the base game. Some models feature specialized systems, such as **custom avionics**, **engine management**, and **flight dynamics**, offering a more challenging and immersive experience.
  - **Real-World Aircraft Replicas**: Some developers create highly detailed replicas of real-world commercial airliners like the **Boeing 747**, **Airbus A380**, or **Lockheed Martin F-22**. These aircraft often come with real-world flight management systems (FMS) and autopilot features, providing you with a real-world airline pilot experience.
- **Helicopters and Special Aircraft**: If you're interested in rotorcraft or military aviation, third-party content includes a wide variety of **helicopters**, **warbirds**, and **experimental planes**. You can practice advanced maneuvers such as hovering, vertical landings, and formation flying, which are vital skills for these types of aircraft.
- **Purchasing Add-ons**: You can find third-party aircraft and models through **marketplaces** such as the **Microsoft Marketplace**, **simMarket**, and

Flightsim.to. Once purchased or downloaded, these aircraft can be installed directly into the simulator and used like the base game's aircraft.

2. Third-Party Scenery and Add-Ons

Another exciting part of the third-party ecosystem is the ability to add **scenery** enhancements to your flights. These add-ons can significantly enhance the realism of specific airports, cities, or entire regions of the world.

- **Photogrammetry Scenery**: Some third-party developers offer **photogrammetry-enhanced cities** and **detailed terrain models**, which improve the realism of landmarks and cities. This makes the flying experience even more immersive when flying over iconic landmarks, such as **New York City** or **Dubai**.

- **Detailed Airports**: Many third-party developers specialize in recreating high-detail airports with accurate runways, taxiways, gates, and ground services. These airports provide better immersion when landing or taking off, with realistic textures and layouts that mirror their real-world counterparts.

- **Weather and Environment Add-Ons**: Third-party developers also create weather packs, lighting systems, and dynamic environment add-ons that can simulate more intense weather phenomena, such as **snowstorms**, **hurricanes**, or

tornadoes, along with **seasonal changes** and real-time **night-time effects**.

3. Realistic Flight Dynamics and Systems Add-ons

For the most advanced simulation experience, third-party developers also offer add-ons that refine **flight dynamics** and aircraft systems.

- **Flight Dynamics Tweaks**: Some developers focus on improving the realism of how aircraft handle during various flight conditions. These tweaks can make your aircraft feel more lifelike and responsive to inputs, replicating the exact characteristics of real-world flying.

- **Avionics Systems Add-ons**: Many third-party content creators offer **realistic avionics systems** that replicate specific models of autopilot, navigation, and weather radar. These systems can enhance your knowledge and experience of flying complex aircraft with real-world instruments.

- **Flight Training Add-ons**: There are specialized training modules created by third-party developers designed to help you master particular skills, such as **aerobatics**, **low-level flying**, or **night flying**. These modules typically include interactive tutorials, checklists, and step-by-step instructions to help you master the craft.

How to Access Extra Training Modules and Resources

For expert pilots who want to take their training further or gain additional resources, *MSFS 2024* offers a range of ways to access specialized training modules and external resources.

1. Using In-Game Training Features

While *MSFS 2024* offers a comprehensive built-in training system, you can expand your training by utilizing advanced features and modules within the simulator:

- **Flight School Add-ons**: Some flight school add-ons provide specialized training tailored to advanced flying skills or specific aircraft. For example, you can find add-ons focused on **long-haul flights, weather-based training, or airline operations**, which simulate real-world aviation scenarios.

- **Mission-Based Training**: These missions help you develop specific skills, such as landing in extreme weather, flying during emergencies, or handling adverse conditions like **high winds** or **fog**. By completing these missions, you gain experience and recognition, making it easier to progress through the more difficult scenarios.

2. Third-Party Training Modules

In addition to in-game content, there are various third-party **training modules** available for download. These modules often offer professional-grade lessons that are more detailed and focused than the general training provided in the base game.

- **Flight Training Schools**: Some developers offer complete virtual flight schools that teach various aviation disciplines, from basic flying to advanced maneuvers. These schools typically provide comprehensive lessons, tutorials, and interactive guidance.

- **Skill-Specific Training**: You can find training modules that focus on specific skills, such as **ILS approaches**, **aerobatic techniques**, or **cross-country navigation**. These modules offer a structured learning path with real-time feedback to help you master each technique.

3. Online Communities and Forums

- **Flight Simulation Forums**: Communities such as **Avsim** and **FlightSim.com** offer a wealth of knowledge and training resources shared by other flight sim enthusiasts. Many experts offer advice, tips, and downloadable resources such as **training PDFs**, **checklists**, and **flight plans**.

- **YouTube and Streaming Platforms**: There are countless flight simulation experts who stream their flights or post instructional videos on platforms like **YouTube**. These videos range from basic tutorials to highly advanced content, such as detailed **airliner operations, real-world flight reviews**, and **advanced IFR procedures**.

Watching others fly can provide valuable insight into new techniques and the latest tools for improving your skills.

- **Flight Sim Schools**: Some organizations offer online, paid **flight simulation training courses** for users who wish to take a structured, professional approach to their flight training. These programs often include private lessons, one-on-one coaching, and certification, allowing you to develop specific skills in a more formal learning environment.

Chapter 12

Expert Tips, Tricks, & Secrets

Whether you're an aspiring pilot or a seasoned aviation enthusiast, *Microsoft Flight Simulator 2024* offers endless opportunities to improve your flying skills. From mastering navigation and performing smooth landings to discovering hidden features and Easter eggs, this section covers expert tips and strategies that will elevate your flight experience.

Pro Tips: Becoming a Master Pilot

Mastering *Microsoft Flight Simulator 2024* requires a combination of technical knowledge, skillful maneuvering, and an understanding of how to maximize the game's features. Here are some pro tips to help you become a master pilot:

1. Mastering the Fundamentals

Before diving into complex maneuvers and high-performance aircraft, it's essential to fully understand the basics of flight:

- **Learn to Fly by Feel**: While instruments are crucial for navigation, learning to feel the aircraft's behavior is key to becoming a skilled pilot. Pay attention to the plane's responses to throttle and control inputs, and practice maintaining smooth, steady flight without constantly relying on the autopilot or instruments.

- **Trim Your Aircraft**: Properly trim your aircraft for level flight to avoid constant input on the yoke or joystick. This makes long flights or cross-country trips much more comfortable. Get used to trimming for different altitudes and airspeeds.

- **Check Your Instruments Regularly**: Regularly scan your **altimeter**, **attitude indicator**, **airspeed indicator**, and **heading indicator** to ensure you're flying within safe parameters. Don't just fly based on the visual cues outside the cockpit.

2. Perfecting Aircraft Control

- **Throttle Control**: Proper throttle management is essential, especially during takeoff, climb, and approach. Learn how to adjust throttle smoothly without causing too much strain on the engine, especially in multi-engine aircraft where fine-tuned power settings are necessary.

- **Controlling the Aircraft in Crosswinds**: Crosswinds can make landings challenging, but learning how to **crab** the aircraft into the wind while maintaining runway alignment is a crucial skill. Practice your crosswind landings by increasing the wind intensity in the weather settings or during multiplayer events.

- **Avoid Overcontrolling**: Overcontrolling your aircraft, especially when flying small planes, can lead to loss of altitude, unsteady flight, or even stalls. Be deliberate and smooth with your control inputs, especially during maneuvers like turns, climbs, or landings.

Expert Strategies for Navigation, Smooth Landings, and More

1. Advanced Navigation Tips

Navigating accurately in *MSFS 2024* is essential, especially during longer flights or when flying in busy airspace. Here are some strategies to make your navigation more precise:

- **Use the GPS and Autopilot Together**: For longer flights, especially in commercial aircraft, the **GPS** system and **autopilot** work hand in hand to reduce pilot workload. Program your route into the GPS system and let the autopilot maintain your heading, altitude, and speed. Keep an eye on the instruments, but trust the systems for long-haul flights.

- **Flight Plans and Waypoints**: When flying in unfamiliar airspace or to unfamiliar destinations, always plan your flight with **waypoints**, **VORs**, and **airways**. Use the **World Map** or flight planning tools in *MSFS 2024* to chart out your route, making navigation easier and more precise.

- **Using ILS for Precision Approaches**: When flying into airports with poor visibility or during night flights, always rely on the **Instrument Landing System (ILS)** for a smooth and precise approach. Learn the approach procedures and adjust your autopilot settings to follow the glide slope and localizer to land safely.

2. Tips for Smooth Landings

Landing smoothly, especially in larger or faster aircraft, requires finesse and proper technique. Follow these tips to make your landings as smooth as possible:

- **Flaps and Speed**: Always ensure you're using the correct **flap settings** for the landing. Most aircraft require 20-40% flaps for the final approach. Also, maintain an appropriate **approach speed**, which is typically indicated in the aircraft's manual or flight performance charts.

- **Approach and Final Approach Setup**: Begin your approach with plenty of time, reducing speed and altitude gradually. Use the autopilot to fly a smooth, constant descent and engage **vertical speed control** for a stable glide slope.

- **The Flare**: As you approach the runway, pull back gently on the yoke or joystick to initiate the **flare**, which lifts the nose of the aircraft and reduces the descent rate. This results in a softer, more controlled landing.

- **Go Around Procedures**: If your approach is too steep or if you miss the runway, don't hesitate to perform a **go-around**. Increase throttle, climb away from the runway, and reconfigure the aircraft for another approach.

Hidden Features and Easter Eggs

In addition to the core flying experience, *Microsoft Flight Simulator 2024* includes several hidden features and Easter eggs that add an extra layer of fun and immersion to the game. Here are a few that you can explore:

1. Hidden Landmarks and Locations

- **The UFO in the Desert**: *MSFS 2024* includes several hidden landmarks, including a UFO crash site in the **Nevada Desert**. If you fly to the coordinates near **Area 51**, you might just spot a crashed UFO surrounded by military vehicles. It's one of many quirky, secret locations scattered around the world.

- **Easter Egg Cities**: There are a number of **Easter egg cities** based on famous fictional locations. For example, you can fly over the city of **Gotham**, or visit **The Shire** from *The Lord of the Rings* series in New Zealand. These are placed strategically across the world map, often hidden in plain sight for players to discover.

2. Easter Eggs in the Sky

- **The Blue Angels**: If you're flying near **Naval Air Stations** or major U.S. military bases, you may catch a glimpse of the **Blue Angels** performing air shows. You can even follow them and perform aerobatic maneuvers with them in multiplayer mode.

- **The Flight Simulator B-17 Bomber**: One fun Easter egg is the **B-17 Bomber** that flies with AI-controlled flight. You might encounter it during certain missions or in multiplayer, and following it allows you to participate in virtual "airshows" or WWII reenactments.

- **The Red Baron's Fokker Dr.1**: If you're flying over certain areas, you might encounter the iconic **Red Baron** flying in his **Fokker Dr.1** triplane, giving you a glimpse into World War I dogfighting history.

3. Secret Weather and Lighting Features

- **Time-of-Day Adjustments**: While the game has a real-time day-night cycle, you can manually adjust the **time-of-day** and **seasonal settings** in the weather menu. Want to see the Northern Lights? Change the season to winter and adjust your location near the poles for a stunning aurora borealis experience.

- **Weather Manipulation for Fun**: You can also manipulate the weather in *MSFS 2024* to create extreme conditions like **hurricanes**, **blizzards**, or **thunderstorms** for extra challenge or to simply experience the power of nature. While this isn't an Easter egg per se, it's a fun secret to experiment with.

Secrets to Enhance Your Flight Experience

To get the most out of your *Microsoft Flight Simulator 2024* experience, here are a few additional tips that can enhance your immersion and overall flying enjoyment:

- **Use Real-Time Live Traffic**: Enable live **real-world air traffic** in multiplayer or solo mode for a fully immersive experience. Watch real-world commercial flights arrive and depart, and adjust your flight plans to avoid busy airspace or join the flight pattern of other aircraft.

- **Enhance Visuals with Add-ons**: Use third-party add-ons to enhance the **scenery** and **lighting** in the game. Custom weather packs, **high-definition cityscapes**, and **photogrammetry** add-ons provide additional realism, especially when flying over famous landmarks or urban areas.

- **Flight Recording and Sharing**: Record your flights and share them with the community. You can even create virtual flight logs and track your progress across missions. This allows you to review your flying techniques, compete with others, and see how you compare in live events or challenges.

- **Exploration Challenges**: Take part in **global challenges**, where you can explore new areas of the world, complete specific missions, or attempt difficult flight conditions. Completing these challenges will improve your skills and earn you rewards in the form of XP, in-game currency, and exclusive aircraft or liveries.

Chapter 13

Troubleshooting & FAQs

Even the most immersive and sophisticated flight simulators like *Microsoft Flight Simulator 2024* can encounter technical issues from time to time. Whether you're experiencing performance issues, setup problems, or encountering bugs, this guide covers common troubleshooting solutions and answers to frequently asked questions to help you enjoy a smoother flying experience.

Technical Support: Solving Common Issues

1. Common Game Crashes or Freezes

- **Possible Causes**:
    - **Outdated Graphics Drivers**: Ensure your **GPU drivers** are up to date, as outdated drivers can cause crashes or performance issues. Check your GPU manufacturer's website (NVIDIA or AMD) for the latest drivers.
    - **Corrupt Game Files**: If the game crashes unexpectedly, it might be due to corrupt or missing game files.

- **Solution**:
    - **Verify Game Files**: If you're using the Microsoft Store or Steam version of *MSFS 2024*, use the **Verify Game Files** option in the store's client to check and repair missing or corrupt files.
    - **Reinstall the Game**: If verification doesn't resolve the issue, you may need to uninstall and then reinstall the game. This ensures that all the necessary files are fresh and intact.

2. **Sim Not Launching or Stuck on Loading Screen**

- **Possible Causes**:
    - **Conflict with Antivirus Software**: Antivirus programs may block or slow down the launch process.
    - **Software Conflicts**: Third-party add-ons or software running in the background could cause the game to hang during startup.
- **Solution**:
    - **Disable Antivirus Temporarily**: Temporarily disable your antivirus program and attempt to launch the game again. You may need to add *MSFS 2024* to your antivirus program's whitelist.

- **Close Background Programs**: Ensure there are no conflicting applications running in the background. Close unnecessary programs (especially those that use the internet, like browsers or download managers) to free up system resources.
- **Run as Administrator**: Right-click on the game's shortcut and select **Run as Administrator** to grant the game proper permissions.

Optimizing Game Performance

Performance can vary depending on your system's specifications. Whether you're experiencing low frame rates, stuttering, or slow loading times, optimizing settings can significantly improve your gaming experience.

1. Adjusting Graphics Settings

- **Lower Graphics Settings**: If your system is struggling with performance, lower the game's graphics settings to improve frame rates:
    - **Reduce Resolution**: Lowering the screen resolution or switching to a windowed mode can improve performance.
    - **Adjust Detail Levels**: Lower settings for **Terrain Detail**, **Object Detail**, **Cloud**

- **Quality**, and **Texture Resolution** to reduce the load on your GPU and improve frame rates.
- ○ **Turn Off Motion Blur**: Disabling motion blur and other post-processing effects like **Depth of Field** can help boost performance.

2. Manage In-Game Traffic and Weather

- **Reduce AI Traffic**: High AI traffic levels (both air and ground) can cause significant performance issues. Lower the AI traffic settings, or switch to a less populated area to see immediate performance improvements.
- **Simplify Weather**: Weather simulations are highly demanding on your system. Simplify weather settings, especially during flights through storms or heavy clouds, to reduce the performance impact.

3. System Optimization

- **Update Drivers**: Ensure that both your **graphics card** and **CPU** drivers are updated. Also, ensure that your **DirectX** installation is up to date.
- **Use Hardware Acceleration**: Make sure that hardware acceleration is enabled in both Windows and in *MSFS 2024*. This will ensure that the game uses your GPU as intended to offload the rendering process from the CPU.

- **Increase Virtual Memory**: If your system is running low on RAM, increasing your **virtual memory (paging file)** in Windows can help. Set it to **1.5 times** your physical RAM for a more responsive experience.

Resolving Controller and Setup Problems

MSFS 2024 supports a wide range of controllers, from joysticks and yokes to pedals and gamepads. However, setting up controllers or troubleshooting connectivity issues can sometimes be tricky.

1. Controller Not Recognized

- **Possible Causes**:
    - **USB Connection Issues**: Controllers may not be recognized if there's a problem with the USB connection.
    - **Driver Issues**: If your controller has outdated or missing drivers, it won't function correctly in *MSFS 2024*.

- **Solution**:
    - **Check USB Ports**: Ensure that your controller is properly plugged into a functional USB port. Try a different port if the controller is not being recognized.
    - **Install/Reinstall Drivers**: For specialized controllers (such as flight yokes, throttle

quadrants, or rudder pedals), ensure that the necessary drivers are installed. Visit the manufacturer's website for the latest drivers and installation instructions.

- o **Check the Controller Settings**: Go into the **Controls** menu in the game and ensure your device is properly configured. You can create and save custom control schemes, so check if your inputs are mapped correctly.

2. Controller Calibration

If you notice that your controller is not responding as expected (for example, the joystick moves the aircraft in a jerky manner), you may need to recalibrate it.

- **Solution**:
    - o **Calibrate in Windows**: Go to **Device Manager**, find your joystick or yoke, and choose **Properties**. Select **Calibrate** to reset the device's input.
    - o **In-Game Calibration**: Use the in-game calibration tool in the **Controls Settings** to calibrate your devices. This ensures that axes (throttle, pitch, yaw, roll) are mapped correctly and operate smoothly.

3. Controller Conflicts

When using multiple input devices (like a joystick and keyboard), there may be conflicts in how controls are mapped.

- **Solution**:
    - **Clear Conflicts**: In the **Controls** menu, ensure that multiple devices are not mapped to the same function (such as throttle or ailerons). You may need to manually unbind specific actions from one controller if they're shared.

Frequently Asked Questions (FAQs)

1. Installation Issues

- **Why can't I install *MSFS 2024*?**
    - Check that you have enough **disk space** available. *MSFS 2024* requires several hundred gigabytes of storage, especially if you have all the world data packs installed.
    - Ensure that your **Windows version** is compatible with the game and that all system requirements are met.
- **The game is stuck during installation. What should I do?**
    - Try **restarting the installation process** or running the installer as **administrator**.

If the issue persists, delete the existing installation files and try again.

2. Game Configurations and Customization

- **How do I customize aircraft controls?**
    - Go to the **Controls Settings** menu to customize the button mappings and axis controls for your devices. You can also save multiple control profiles for different aircraft and adjust settings for each flight.

- **Can I adjust the in-game weather for specific flights?**
    - Yes, you can manually adjust weather conditions through the **Weather Menu** during flight planning or mid-flight. You can choose preset weather conditions or create custom scenarios for specific challenges.

3. Performance and Graphics

- **Why is my frame rate low during flight?**
    - Check your **graphics settings** and adjust them for better performance. You may need to lower **resolution**, **terrain detail**, or **cloud quality** if your system is struggling to maintain a high frame rate.

- **How can I improve loading times for large airports?**

- Consider reducing the **airport detail level** and **AI traffic** to improve load times. You can also install scenery and airport add-ons that are optimized for better performance.

Conclusion & Final Thoughts

Microsoft Flight Simulator 2024 offers an unparalleled aviation experience, combining stunning realism, rich detail, and immersive gameplay. Whether you're a seasoned pilot or a newcomer to flight simulators, *MSFS 2024* provides the tools and features to expand your skills and explore the world from above like never before.

Take Off: Your Next Adventure Awaits

Now that you're equipped with expert tips, troubleshooting insights, and guidance for enhancing your flying skills, it's time to take off and embark on your next great adventure. The world is your runway, and *MSFS 2024* offers endless opportunities to explore, learn, and challenge yourself in the skies.

- **Start with Training**: If you're new to flight simulators or want to hone specific skills, use the interactive training modules to master the basics, work through advanced maneuvers, or even tackle complex commercial airliners.

- **Join the Multiplayer Community**: Connect with other pilots in the multiplayer mode, participate in live events, or engage in global challenges for a truly immersive and social experience.

- **Explore New Horizons**: With live weather, real-time traffic, and the ability to customize your aircraft and environment, every flight in *MSFS 2024* promises something unique. Use the world map to plan your next journey, whether it's flying over iconic landmarks, tackling a difficult landing, or experiencing a dynamic weather system.

Your flight experience doesn't end here—there's always a new challenge, new mission, or new destination to discover. The skies are waiting.

Recap of Essential Tips and Information

Before you soar, here's a quick recap of some essential takeaways to ensure a smooth flying experience:

- **Master the Basics**: Focus on controlling your aircraft with smooth inputs, trimming for stable flight, and using instruments to monitor speed, altitude, and heading.

- **Flight Planning**: Use the world map for flight planning and make sure to adjust for weather, air traffic, and potential hazards. Familiarize yourself with the navigation aids (VOR, GPS, ILS) to ensure accurate route following.

- **Weather Awareness**: The dynamic live weather system adds realism but also presents challenges. Use weather data for route planning, and adapt during flights by adjusting altitude, speed, and approach based on the conditions.

- **Master Landings**: Landing can be tricky—always ensure that you've reduced speed, adjusted for

- crosswinds, and practiced smooth flare techniques. Use autopilot features like ILS to help with precision landings in challenging conditions.

- **Troubleshooting**: If you encounter issues like crashes, performance drops, or controller malfunctions, use the troubleshooting steps to optimize performance and resolve technical problems. Keep your drivers updated, optimize game settings, and calibrate your controllers for smoother control.

With these essentials, you're ready to take to the skies confidently, no matter what type of aircraft or flying conditions you encounter.

Looking Ahead: What's Next for Microsoft Flight Simulator?

As *Microsoft Flight Simulator 2024* continues to evolve, there are exciting updates and expansions on the horizon. The developers at Asobo Studio and the community continue to push the boundaries of what's possible in a flight simulation game, ensuring that *MSFS 2024* remains at the forefront of immersive flying experiences.

1. Future Updates and Expansions

- **New Aircraft**: Expect additional aircraft models, both official and third-party, to be added over time. These updates may include new commercial airliners, military aircraft, and even experimental planes.

- **Enhanced Weather Systems**: The live weather system is continually refined, with future updates expected to improve cloud rendering, atmospheric conditions, and the way weather impacts flight dynamics.

- **Advanced Flight Systems**: As the game grows, expect more sophisticated autopilot systems, flight management tools, and avionics that will allow for even deeper realism, especially in commercial aviation.

- **New Regions and Scenery Packs**: With *MSFS 2024's* expansive world, there's always more to explore. Future updates will likely bring more detailed photogrammetry models for cities, rural areas, and even remote locations around the world, enhancing the sense of exploration.

2. Community Projects and Add-Ons

- **Community-Driven Content**: One of the most exciting aspects of *MSFS 2024* is its dedicated community. Players and third-party developers are constantly working to add new features, scenery, aircraft, and training modules. Whether you're looking for new flight missions or specialized aircraft, the community continually provides exciting add-ons.

- **Shared Multiplayer Events**: The game will continue to host live events, seasonal challenges, and global flights that bring together pilots from all over the world. These events are an excellent way to connect with fellow flight enthusiasts and test your skills.

- **Custom Mods and Enhancements**: Third-party content creators regularly release mods that add new challenges, change the gameplay experience, or enhance visual realism. Keep an eye on the modding community for the latest tools, like custom airports, aircraft, or realistic environmental effects.

3. Virtual Reality (VR) and Future Technology

As VR technology advances, *MSFS 2024* is expected to continue its integration with virtual reality headsets, allowing for even more immersive experiences. Whether flying from the cockpit of an airliner or piloting a small GA plane through the mountains, VR will take your flight sim experience to the next level.

www.ingramcontent.com/pod-product-compliance
Lightning Source LLC
Chambersburg PA
CBHW052259220526
45471CB00001B/404